IV. double consonant sound

Double consonant sounds are indicated by a small 「つ [tsu]」 preceding the "kana" containing the Consonant sound. This 「つ [tsu]」 means that the following consonant is to be given two syllables' duration.

きっぷ kippu : ticket	けっこん kekkon : marriage
ざっし zasshi : magazine	せっけん sekken : soap

V. a long vowel [sound]

a + a → aa	i + i → ii	u + u → uu
あぁ → aa (a a)	いい → ii (i i)	うう → uu (u u)
かぁ → kaa (ka a)	きい → kii (ki i)	くう → kuu (ku u)
さぁ → saa (sa a)	しい → shii (si i)	すう → suu (su u)
たぁ → taa (ta a)	ちい → chii (ti i)	つう → tsuu (tsu u)
なぁ → naa (na a)	にい → nii (ni i)	ぬう → nuu (nu u)
はぁ → haa (ha a)	ひい → hii (hi i)	ふう → fuu (fu u)
まぁ → maa (ma a)	みい → mii (mi i)	むう → muu (mu u)
やぁ → yaa (ya a)		ゆう → yuu (yu u)
らぁ → raa (ra a)	りい → rii (ri i)	るう → ruu (ru u)
わぁ → waa (wa a)		

e + e ee	e + i ee	o + o oo	o + u oo
ええ → ee (e e)	えい → ee (e i)	おお → oo (o o)	おう → oo (o u)
けえ → kee (ke e)	けい → kee (ke i)	こお → koo (ko o)	こう → koo (ko u)
せえ → see (se e)	せい → see (se i)	そお → soo (so o)	そう → soo (so u)
てえ → tee (te e)	てい → tee (te i)	とお → too (to o)	とう → too (to u)
ねえ → nee (ne e)	ねい → nee (ne i)	のお → noo (no o)	のう → noo (no u)
へえ → hee (he e)	へい → hee (he i)	ほお → hoo (ho o)	ほう → hoo (ho u)
めえ → mee (me e)	めい → mee (me i)	もお → moo (mo o)	もう → moo (mo u)
		よお → yoo (yo o)	よう → yoo (yo u)
れえ → ree (re e)	れい → ree (re i)	ろお → roo (ro o)	ろう → roo (ro u)

おねえさん oneesan : elder sister	とけい tokee : watch, clock
こおり koori : ice	ぼうし booshi : hat, cap

H. TOKUMOTO
H. YAMAMOTO
K. SUZUKI

SURVIVAL JAPANESE

FOR UNIVERSITY STUDENTS

1

---Intellectual and effective approach for beginners---

SOBI-SHUPPANSHA

この教科書をお使いになる方へ

　進展するグローバル化に伴い、日本語をほとんど学んだことのない状態で来日する大学生・大学院生が増えています。また、日本にいながら日本語がまったくわからなくても英語だけで学位が取れる大学のコースも増えてきました。そのため、従来の日本語専攻の学生を主対象とするアカデミックな日本語教育とは趣の異なる日本語教育が必要とされるようになり、多くの大学でそのようなニーズに応えた日本語クラスを設置するようになってきました。

　名古屋大学、三重大学及び愛知教育大学の３大学でも、文部科学省の「平成24年度大学改革強化推進事業」に採択された「アジアを中心とする国際人材育成と大学連携による国際化の加速度的推進事業」に基づき、2013年度から理工系大学院で学ぶ留学生向けサバイバル日本語講座を開設することになり、名古屋外国語大学がその開設・運営について協力依頼を受けて、国立３大学連携日本語講座として2013年度から3年に渡り開講・実施しました。受講生は理系分野を専門とする大学院生で研究に日本語は必要とされておらず、日本語は課外で学ばねばなりませんでした。学習意欲は旺盛ですが学習時間が限られた彼らを対象に、大学生活に即した実用的な日本語を効果的に教えるために書き下ろしたテキストが、この教科書の基となっています。

　今回の出版にあたり、語彙や場面などを差し替えて汎用性を持たせ、理系文系に関係なく、大学生および大学院生が日本で快適な留学生活を送るための日本語を学ぶことができる教科書として書き直しました。サバイバル教科書にありがちな場面シラバス一本槍ではなく文法シラバスを下敷きにし、表面的には日本での大学生活でしばしば遭遇する場面を扱っています。大人の場合、場面シラバスだけではなかなか応用が利かず、学習にストレスを感じるようになることが多くあります。そこで、文法シラバスと場面シラバスを組み合わせた上で、学習者がよく使うと思われる大きな語彙リストを付与しました。そうすることで、学習者は、教科書としてだけではなく、参考書や辞書としてもこの教科書を使うことができます。この教科書が手元にあると学生生活および研究生活における最低限の会話ができるようになることを狙っています。

　この教科書がみなさんが日本で快適な留学生活を送るための助けとなることを、著者一同願っています。

著　者

この教科書について

対象

この教科書は、日本語を学んだことのない人を対象にしています。特に以下のような人にふさわしい内容となっています。

- サバイバル日本語を効果的に速習したい人
- 日本での留学および研究生活を快適にするためにサバイバル日本語を学びたい学生およびその家族
- 初級日本語の概要をつかみたい学生

レベル

日本語を学んだことのない、あるいはほとんどない学習者の学習意欲を高め、即運用につながる実践的な力を養うことを狙いとして、Can-doシラバスを採用しました。Can-doは国際交流基金のJFスタンダードで示されているレベルのA1相当を基本としています。日本語を専門的に学ぶわけではなく、日本の大学で一定期間を過ごすために最低限必要な力ということで、このレベルを選定しました。

巻末の語彙索引は、留学生として大学生活や日常生活を送るために最低限必要と思われる語彙を中心に選定しました。これらの語彙は旧日本語能力試験4級レベルの約60%をカバーしています。

構成

本書は1課から15課まであります。Volume 1は1課から8課まで、Volume 2は9課から15課までをカバーしています。学習時間は、1課を2〜4時間で修了し、全15課で30〜60時間を想定しています。週1回の学習であっても、1課を2時間ペースで進めるなら、15週つまり大学の半期間で全課修了できる構成です。少しゆっくり進めたとしても、大学の1年で全課修了できます。

構成は以下のようになっています。また下記に加え、課毎の語彙・表現リスト（和文ローマ字併記：英訳付）が別冊として付属し、MCとCEの音声ファイルもオンラインで無償提供されています。

— ii —

```
場面ごとのモデル会話（MC）
      ↓
Structure Exercises（SE）：oral
      ↓
Conversational Exercises（CE）            各課の構成（1課～15課）
      ↓                                  （すべて和文ローマ字併記）
Structure Exercises（SE）：writing
```
↓

文法解説（英文）

↓

索引： Can-do、文型および語彙索引（和文ローマ字併記）
  ➤ 語彙索引には、カテゴリー別の語彙リスト（動詞、形容詞、場所、食べ
    物＆飲み物：英訳付）も付属

この教科書の使い方

● MCは、研究室や寮など学生生活に関係がある場面での会話です。初級語彙ながら自然な
  会話に近づけた内容となっています。また、場面が大学生活に即したものになっているた
  め、座学だけではなく、教室外におけるアクティビティにも使いやすいものとなっていま
  す。各課の内容を学習したあとで使えば、より実践的な応用練習ができます。

● SE：oralは、語彙・語順・語形など、正確に話すための練習です。Yes/No Questionや疑
  問詞Questionといったいろいろなパターンの質問に正確に答える練習もできます。ここで
  しっかり基礎を固めます。

● CEは適切に話す練習です。小会話ながらそれぞれに場面が設定されており、その場面にふ
  さわしい語彙・文法の使い方や文末表現、あいづちなどのストラテジーの練習ができま
  す。この練習で実際の場面でも話せるように自信をつけます。

● MCは、語彙・SE：oral・CEの練習の後、内容理解・表現・イントネーション等、総合的
  に運用能力を上げるための練習に再度使うことができます。

● SE：writingは、話す練習の後で、文法や表現の確認をしながら学習したことを定着させる
  練習です。

About This Textbook

Target

● This textbook is for beginners of Japanese and especially perfect for the following students.

♦ Students who want to learn survival Japanese quickly but effectively

♦ International students in Japan and their family who want to lead their lives in Japan smoothly and comfortably

♦ Students who want to grasp the essence of beginners' Japanese

Level

● This textbook conforms to JF Standard Level A1 of Japan Foundation, which is the minimum level of Japanese to live in Japan comfortably as international students. In the Study Target index at the back of the book, what students are expected to become able to do using Japanese in each lesson is listed.

● This textbook covers about 60% of Level 4 vocabularies of old Japanese Language Proficiency Test.

Design

● This textbook has 15 lessons. Volume 1 covers from Lesson 1 to 8 and Volume 2 from Lesson 8 to 15. Students are expected to finish each lesson in 2 to 4 hours and the entire textbook in 30 to 60 hours. That means students are able to finish both the volumes in one semester even if the class meets only once a week, if the class pace is 2 hours per lesson. Even when the class pace is a little slower, students can finish both the volumes in one school year comfortably.

● Each lesson introduces Model Conversation (MC) in the typical situation that university students often encounter. "Structure Exercises (SE) : oral", "Conversational Exercises (CE)" and "Structure Exercises (SE) : writing" will follow MC. Refer to the flow chart below. Each lesson has the set of these 4 sections and they are expected to be covered in class.

● Grammar Notes and Indexes (Study Target, Structure, and Vocabulary) are provided at the back of the book. Vocabulary and expression lists by lessons are also given as a separate booklet for the convenience of learners.

● Grammar Notes are written all in English and students are able to study this section on their own.

● Except Grammar Notes, this textbook is all written in both Hiragana and Roma-ji (Roman alphabet) so that students can start studying structures even before mastering Japanese writing system.

● Vocabulary index has the lists by word categories (verbs, adjectives, places, foods & drinks).

● Audio files for MC and CE are available online free of charge.

— iv —

Model Conversation （MC）
↓
Structure Exercises （SE） : oral
↓
Conversational Exercises （CE）
↓
Structure Exercises （SE） : writing

Each Lesson (Lesson 1～15)

↓
Grammar Notes
↓
Indexes (Study Target, Structure, and Vocabulary)

How to Use this Textbook

- MC adopts typical and real situations for university students such as dormitory, research lab, etc. and can be used not only in class but also for activities outside classroom easily.
- Even though MC uses only simple vocabularies, the conversation is natural so that students can apply MC in practical situations easily. It is a good example of Japanese as it's really spoken.
- Once vocabulary practice, SE, and CE are done, MC helps students to deepen their understanding of Japanese structure and to improve their overall ability to use proper expressions and intonations effectively.
- SE(oral) is a practice of vocabularies, word orders, verb forms, etc. in order to speak accurately. Students can also practice how to answer various questions properly. Students are expected to make the solid foundation of structures here for the next step.
- CE is a practice of speaking properly. Even though they are short conversations, they are all set in the appropriate situations. Students are able to learn vocabularies and grammar suitable for each situation. We hope students gain confidence to speak in Japanese after this practice.
- SE(wring) is used to master what has studied so far while confirming the structure and expressions introduced in the lesson,

— v —

SURVIVAL JAPANESE
FOR UNIVERSITY STUDENTS
も　く　じ
Contents

あいさつ Greetings

Classroom Expressions 2

Everyday Greetings and Expressions 4

Aisatsu Greetings

Classroom Expressions 3

Everyday Greetings and Expressions 5

Lesson 1

じこしょうかい Self-Introduction

Model Conversation 6

Structural Exercises : oral 8

Conversational Exercises 12

Structural Exercices : writing 16

Lesson 1

Jikoshookai Self-Introduction

Model Conversation 7

Structural Exercises : oral 9

Conversational Exercises 13

Structural Exercices : writing 17

Lesson 2

きょうしつで (1) In the Classroom (1)

Model Conversation 20

Structural Exercises : oral 22

Conversational Exercises 26

Structural Exercices : writing 28

Lesson 2

Kyooshitsu de (1) In the Classroom (1)

Model Conversation 21

Structural Exercises : oral 23

Conversational Exercises 27

Structural Exercices : writing 29

Lesson 3

パーティで At a Party

Model Conversation 34

Structural Exercises : oral 36

Conversational Exercises 42

Structural Exercices : writing 44

Lesson 3

Paatii de At a Party

Model Conversation 35

Structural Exercises : oral 37

Conversational Exercises 43

Structural Exercices : writing 45

Lesson 4

みせで At a Shop

Model Conversation 48

Structural Exercises : oral 50

Conversational Exercises 54

Structural Exercices : writing 56

Lesson 4

Mise de At a Shop

Model Conversation 49

Structural Exercises : oral 51

Conversational Exercises 55

Structural Exercices : writing 57

SURVIVAL JAPANESE
FOR UNIVERSITY STUDENTS
も　く　じ
Contents

Lesson 5
テスト　Exam

Model Conversation	60
Structural Exercises : oral	62
Conversational Exercises	68
Structural Exercices : writing	74

Lesson 5
Tesuto　Exam

Model Conversation	61
Structural Exercises : oral	63
Conversational Exercises	69
Structural Exercices : writing	75

Lesson 6
はっぴょう Presentation

Model Conversation	80
Structural Exercises : oral	82
Conversational Exercises	86
Structural Exercices : writing	88

Lesson 6
Happyoo　Presentationn

Model Conversation	81
Structural Exercises : oral	83
Conversational Exercises	87
Structural Exercices : writing	89

Lesson 7
しょうたい　Invitation

Model Conversation	94
Structural Exercises : oral	96
Conversational Exercises	98
Structural Exercices : writing	...100

Lesson 7
Shootai　Invitation

Model Conversation	95
Structural Exercises : oral	97
Conversational Exercises	99
Structural Exercices : writing	...101

Lesson 8
わたしのかぞく（1） My Family (1)

Model Conversation	...104
Structural Exercises : oral	...106
Conversational Exercises	...110
Structural Exercices : writing	...114

Lesson 8
Watashi no Kazoku (1) My Family (1)

Model Conversation	...105
Structural Exercises : oral	...107
Conversational Exercises	...111
Structural Exercices : writing	...115

アクティビティ　Activity	120
ぶんぽうノート　Grammer Notes	121
ターゲット インデックス　Study Target Index	...153
ぶんぽう インデックス　Structure Index	155

ごい インデックス　Vocabulary Index	157
さくいん　　Index by Hiragana sounds	162
かいとう　Answers (Structual Exercises : writing)	170

ごい・ひょうげん　Vocabulary・Expressions ...べっさつ booklet

Characters

ハイン[Hain]
ベトナム [betonamu]
法学 [hoogaku]
Hein
Vietnam / law

チン[Chin]
中国 [chuugoku]
化学 [kagaku]
Chen
China / chemistry

アン[An]
タイ [tai]
物理 [butsuri]
An
Thai / physics

ブディ[Budi]
マレーシア [mareeshia]
コンピューター [kon'pyuutaa]
Budhi
Malaysia / computer

さとう[Satoo]
日本 [nihon]
物理 [butsuri]
Sato
Japan / physics

もり[Mori]
日本 [nihon]
物理 [butsuri]
Mori
Japan / physics

たかはし[Takahashi]
日本 [nihon]
コンピューター [kon'pyuutaa]
Takahashi
Japan / computer

ミン[Min]
ベトナム [betonamu]
経済 [keezai]
Minh
Vietnam / economy

あんどう[Andoo]
助手 [joshu]
Ando
secretary

たなか[Tanaka]
先生 [sensee]
Tanaka
professor

なかむら[Nakamura]
先生 [sensee]
Nakamura
professor

SURVIVAL JAPANESE

FOR UNIVERSITY STUDENTS

1

Useful Expressions

あいさつ
Greetings

Targets :
- ✓ Can read his/her name, country name, and a field of study.
- ✓ Can understand and follow short and simple classroom instructions from the teacher such as "please listen" "please read" if the speech is slow and clear.
- ✓ Can make basic greetings appropriate to the situation to a friend or a neighbor.

Classroom Expressions : ⓪1

1. なまえ
2. しゅくだい
3. しつもん
4. こたえ
5. れい
6. はじめましょう。
7. おわりましょう。
8. やすみましょう。
9. わかりますか。/わかりました。/わかりません。
10. きいて ください。
11. みて ください。
12. よんで ください。
13. かいて ください。
14. いって ください。
15. きて ください。
16. もう いちど。
17. いいです。
18. ちがいます。

Useful Expressions

Aisatsu
Greetings

Targets :
- ✓ Can read his/her name, country name, and a field of study.
- ✓ Can understand and follow short and simple classroom instructions from the teacher such as "please listen" "please read" if the speech is slow and clear.
- ✓ Can make basic greetings appropriate to the situation to a friend or a neighbor.

Classroom Expressions : ⓪①

1. namae
2. shukudai
3. shitsumon
4. kotae
5. ree
6. Hajimemashoo.
7. Owarimashoo.
8. Yasumimashoo.
9. Wakarimasu ka. / Wakarimashita. / Wakarimasen.
10. Kiite kudasai.
11. Mite kudasai.
12. Yon'de kudasai.
13. Kaite kudasai.
14. Itte kudasai.
15. Kite kudasai.
16. Moo ichi-do.
17. Ii desu.
18. Chigaimasu.

Everyday Greetings and Expressions : ⓪2

1. おはようございます。

2. こんにちは。

3. こんばんは。

4. さようなら。

5. ありがとうございます。

6. すみません。

7. おねがいします。

8. しつれいします。

9. じゃ、また。

Everyday Greetings and Expressions : ⑫

1. Ohayoo gozaimasu.

2. Kon'nichiwa.

3. Kon'banwa.

4. Sayoonara.

5. Arigatoo gozaimasu.

6. Sumimasen.

7. Onegaishimasu.

8. Shitsureeshimasu.

9. Ja, mata.

Lesson 1

じこしょうかい
Self-Introduction

Targets:
- ✓ Can provide your own name, hometown, field of study, etc. to a person you have just met.
- ✓ Can ask a person around you for his / her name, hometown, field of study, etc. or give such information when asked.

Model Conversation :

ブディ　　：　こんにちは。ブディです。マレーシアから　きました。
　　　　　　　よろしく　おねがいします。
たかはし　：　はじめまして。たかはしです。
　　　　　　　ブディさん、せんもんは　ぶつりですか。
ブディ　　：　いいえ、せんもんは　コンピューターです。
たかはし　：　わたしも　コンピューターです。
　　　　　　　これから　いっしょに　けんきゅうします。
　　　　　　　よろしく　おねがいします。

Lesson 1

Jikoshookai
Self-Introduction

Targets:
- ✓ Can provide your own name, hometown, field of study, etc. to a person you have just met.
- ✓ Can ask a person around you for his/her name, hometown, field of study, etc. or give such information when asked.

Model Conversation : 03

Budi : Kon'nichiwa. Budi desu. Mareeshia kara kimashita.
　　　　Yoroshiku onegaishimasu.
Takahashi : Hajimemashite. Takahashi desu.
　　　　Budi-san, sen'mon wa keezai desu ka.
Budi : Iie, sen'mon wa kon'pyuutaa desu.
Takahashi : Watashi mo kon'pyuutaa desu.
　　　　Kore kara issho ni ken'kyuushimasu.
　　　　Yoroshiku onegaishimasu.

Structural Exercises : oral

1

れい） 1. ハインさんは　ベトナムじんです。
2. A：ハインさんは　がくせいですか。
   B：はい、がくせいです。
3. A：ハインさんは　がくせいです。あんどうさんも　がくせいですか。
   B：いいえ、がくせいじゃ　ありません。じょしゅです。

2

れい）　A：あのひとは　だれ（どなた）ですか。
　　　B：ブディさんです。

1) アンさん
2) ミンさん
3) きむらせんせい
4) せんぱいの　たかはしさん

Structural Exercises : oral

1

e.g.) 1. <u>Hain-san</u> wa <u>betonamu-jin</u> desu.

2. A : <u>Hain-san</u> wa <u>gakusee</u> desu ka.

   B : Hai, <u>gakusee</u> desu.

3. A : Hain-san wa <u>gakusee</u> desu. An'doo-san mo <u>gakusee</u> desu ka.

   B : Iie, <u>gakusee</u> ja' arimasen. <u>Joshu</u> desu.

2

e.g.)   A : Ano hito wa dare (donata) desu ka.

   B : <u>Budi-san</u> desu.

1) An-san
2) Min-san
3) Kimura sen'see
4) Sen'pai no Takahashi-san

3

れい）　A：すみません。あの　ひとは　どなたですか。
　　　B：①もりさんです。
　　　A：①もりさんは　②せんせいですか。
　　　B：いいえ、②せんせいじゃ　ありません。③がくせいです。

1)　① あんどうさん　② がくせい　　　　③ じょしゅ
2)　① ブディさん　　② がくせい　　　　③ こうかんりゅうがくせい
3)　① アンさん　　　② だいがくいんせい　③ けんきゅうせい

4

みなさん、はじめまして。ブディです。
マレーシアから　きました。
にっしんだいの　がくせいです。
せんもんは　コンピューターです。
よろしく　おねがいします。

みなさん、はじめまして。＿＿＿＿＿＿＿＿＿＿です。
＿＿＿＿＿＿＿＿＿＿から　きました。
＿＿＿＿＿＿＿＿＿＿の　＿＿＿＿＿＿＿＿＿＿です。
せんもんは　＿＿＿＿＿＿＿＿＿＿です。
よろしく　おねがいします。

3

e.g.) A : Sumimasen. Ano hito wa donata desu ka.
       B : ①Mori-san desu.
       A : ①Mori-san wa ②sen'see desu ka.
       B : Iie, ②sen'see ja' arimasen. ③gakusee desu.

1) ① An'doo-san   ② gakusee   ③ joshu
2) ① Budi-san   ② gakusee   ③ kookan ryuugakusee
3) ① An-san   ② daigakuin'see ③ ken'kyuusee

4

Mina-san, hajimemashite. Budi desu.
Mareeshia kara kimashita.
Nisshin'dai no gakusee desu.
Sen'mon wa kon'pyuutaa desu.
Yoroshiku onegaishimasu.

Mina-san, hajimemashite. _____ desu.
_____ kara kimashita.
_____ no _____ desu.
Sen'mon wa _____ desu.
Yoroshiku onegaishimasu.

Conversational Exercises :

1. ブディ：すみません。あの　ひとは　どなたですか。
⑭　さとう：①ミンさんです。
　　ブディ：①ミンさんは　②けんきゅうせいですか。
　　さとう：いいえ、②けんきゅうせいじゃ　ありません。③だいがくいんせいです。
　　ブディ：そうですか。

　　1) ①よしださん　　②じむの　ひと　　③ドクターの　せんぱい
　　2) ①チンさん　　　②ここの　がくせい　③あおぞらだいがくの　がくせい

2. アン　：①ハインさんは　②ベトナムじんですか。
⑮　ミン　：はい、そうです。
　　アン　：③ブディさんも　②ベトナムじんですか。
　　ミン　：いいえ、③ブディさんは　マレーシアじんです。

　　1) ①チンさん　　②ちゅうごくじん　　③リュウさん
　　2) ①ヨウさん　　②かんこくじん　　　③ワンさん

Conversational Exercises:

1. Budi : Sumimasen. Ano hito wa donata desu ka.
④ Satoo : ① <u>Min-san</u> desu.
Budi : ① <u>Min-san</u> wa ② <u>ken'kyuusee</u> desu ka.
Satoo : Iie, ② <u>ken'kyuusee</u> ja' arimasen. ③ <u>Daigakuin'see</u> desu.
Budi : Soo desu ka.

1) ① Yoshida-san   ② jimu no hito   ③ dokutaa no sen'pai
2) ① Chin-san   ② koko no gakusee ③ Aozora Daigaku no gakusee

2. An   : ① <u>Hain-san</u> wa ② <u>Betonamu-jin</u> desu ka.
⑤ Minh : Hai, soo desu.
An   : ③ <u>Budi-san</u> mo ② <u>Betonamu-jin</u> desu ka.
Minh : Iie, ③ <u>Budi-san</u> wa Mareeshia-jin desu.

1) ① Chin-san   ② Chuugoku-jin   ③ Ryuu-san
2) ① Yoo-san   ② Kan'koku-jin   ③ Wan-san

— 13 —

3.
⑥
たかはし ：あ、ブディさん、こんにちは。
ブディ　　：こんにちは。あの、しつれいですが・・・・。
たかはし ：<u>たかはし</u>です。
ブディ　　：<u>たかはし</u>さん・・・
たかはし ：はい、そうです。よろしく　おねがいします。
ブディ　　：はい、よろしく　おねがいします。

1) あんどう
2) さとう

4.
⑦
あんどう：ブディさん、こちらは　①<u>ハイン</u>さんです。
　　　　　①<u>ハイン</u>さん、こちらは　ブディさんです。
　　　　　ブディさんも　②<u>ここ</u>の　がくせいです。
ブディ　　：はじめまして。ブディです。
①<u>ハイン</u>：ブディさん、はじめまして。①<u>ハイン</u>です。
　　　　　どうぞ　よろしく　おねがいします。
ブディ　　：こちらこそ　よろしく　おねがいします。

1) ①チン　　　　②にっしんだいがく
2) ①たかはし　　②コンピューター

3.
Takahashi : A, Budi-san, kon'nichiwa.
Budi : Kon'nichiwa. Ano, shitsuree desu ga….
Takahashi : <u>Takahashi</u> desu.
Budi : <u>Takahashi</u>-san ….
Takahashi : Hai, soo desu. Yoroshiku onegaishimasu.
Budi : Hai, yoroshiku onegaishimasu.

1) An'doo
2) Satoo

4.
An'doo : Budi-san, kochira wa ①<u>Hain</u>-san desu.
　　　　　①<u>Hain</u>-san, kochira wa Budi-san desu.
　　　　　Budi-san mo ② <u>koko</u> no gakusee desu.
Budi : Hajimemashite. Budi desu.
①<u>Hain</u> : Budi-san, hajimemashite. ① <u>Hain</u> desu.
　　　　Doozo yoroshiku onegaishimasu.
Budi : Kochira koso yoroshiku onegaishimasu.

1) ① Chin　　② Nisshin Daigaku
2) ① Takahashi　② kon'pyuutaa

Structural Exercices : writing

1. れい)【 ブディ ・ です ・ は ・ わたし 】

   → <u> わたしは　ブディです。 </u>

1)【 か ・ アンさん ・ です ・ いんせい ・ も 】

   → _____

2)【 にほんじん ・ は ・ じゃ ありません ・ ハインさん 】

   → _____

3)【 から ・ わたし ・ マレーシア ・ は ・ きました 】

   → _____

4)【 ジョンさん ・ の ・ にっしんだいがく ・ です ・ だいがくいんせい ・ は 】

   → _____

2. れい)【 がくせい ・ もり ・ せんせい 】

   A：すみません。あの　ひとは　どなたですか。

   B：<u>　もりさん　</u>です。

   A：<u>　もりさん　</u>は　せんせいですか。

   B：いいえ、<u>　せんせい　</u>じゃ　ありません。<u>　がくせい　</u>です。

1)　【 じょしゅ ・ あんどうさん ・ いんせい 】

   A：すみません。あの　ひとは　どなたですか。

   B：_____です。

   A：_____は　いんせいですか。

   B：いいえ、_____じゃ　ありません。_____です。

2)　【 ミンさん ・ ベトナム ・ タイ 】

   A：アンさんは　タイじんですか。

   B：はい、そうです。

   A：_____も_____じんですか。

   B：いいえ、_____は_____じんです。

Structural Exercices : writing

1. e.g.) 【Budi ・ desu ・ wa ・ watashi 】

→ Watashi wa Budi desu.

1) 【ka ・ An-san ・ desu ・ in'see ・ mo 】

→_____

2) 【Nihon-jin ・ wa ・ ja'arimasen ・ Hain-san 】

→_____

3) 【kara ・ watashi ・ Mareeshia ・ wa ・ kimashita 】

→_____

4) 【Jon-san ・ no ・ Nisshin Daigaku ・ desu ・ daigakuin'see ・ wa 】

→_____

2. e.g.) 【gakusee ・ Mori ・ sen'see 】

A : Sumimasen. Ano hito wa donata desu ka.

B : _Mori-san_ desu.

A : _Mori-san_ wa sen'see desu ka.

B : Iie, _sen'see_ ja' arimasen. _Gakusee_ desu.

1) 【joshu ・ An'doo-san ・ in'see 】

A : Sumimasen. Ano hito wa donata desu ka.

B : _____ desu.

A : _____ wa in'see desu ka.

B : Iie, _____ ja' arimasen. _____ desu.

2) 【Min-san ・ Betonamu ・ Tai 】

A : An-san wa Tai-jin desu ka.

B : Hai, soo desu.

A : _____ mo _____-jin desu ka.

B : Iie, _____ wa _____-jin desu.

— 17 —

3) 【 ぶつり ・ そう ・ コンピューター 】

A：アンさんは　だいがくいんせいですか。

B：はい、＿＿＿＿＿＿＿＿＿です。

A：せんもんは　コンピューターですか。

B：いいえ、＿＿＿＿＿＿＿＿＿じゃ　ありません。

　　せんもんは＿＿＿＿＿＿＿＿＿です。

4) 【 だいがくいんせい ・ コンピューター ・ たかはし 】

みなさん、はじめまして。＿＿＿＿＿＿＿＿＿です。

にっしんだいの＿＿＿＿＿＿＿＿＿です。

せんもんは＿＿＿＿＿＿＿＿＿です。

これから　いっしょに　けんきゅうします。よろしく　おねがいします。

5) 【 ほうがく ・ ハイン ・ ベトナム 】

みなさん、はじめまして。＿＿＿＿＿＿＿＿＿です。

＿＿＿＿＿＿＿＿＿から　きました。

せんもんは　＿＿＿＿＿＿＿＿＿　です。よろしく　おねがいします。

3) 【 butsuri ・ soo ・ kon'pyuutaa 】

    A : An-san wa daigakuin'see desu ka.

    B : Hai, _____ desu.

    A : Sen'mon wa kon'pyuutaa desu ka.

    B : Iie, _____ ja' arimasen.

        Sen'mon wa_____ desu.

4) 【 daigakuin'see ・ kon'pyuutaa ・ Takahashi 】

    Mina-san, hajimemashite. _____ desu.

    Nisshin'dai no _____ desu.

    Sen'mon wa _____ desu.

    Kore kara issho ni ken'kyuushimasu. Yoroshiku onegaishimasu.

5) 【 hoogaku ・ Hain ・ Betonamu 】

    Mina-san, hajimemashite. _____desu.

    _____ kara kimashita.

    Sen'mon wa _____ desu. Yoroshiku onegaishimasu.

— 19 —

Lesson 2

きょうしつで（1）
In the Classroom (1)

Targets :
- ✓ Can ask and answer to whom something belongs.
- ✓ Can exchange phone numbers with someone.
- ✓ Can express agreement or confirmation.

Model Conversation : ⑧

＜In the Classroom＞

たかはし： ブディさん、それは　なんですか。
ブディ　： これですか。はっぴょうの　しりょうです。
たかはし： へえ、ブディさんのですか。
ブディ　： いいえ、ミンさんのです。
たかはし： ミンさん？どなたですか。
ブディ　： ミンさんは　りょうの　ともだちです。ベトナムじんです。
たかはし： そうですか。

Lesson 2

Kyooshitsu de（1）
In the Classroom（1）

Targets :
- ✓ Can ask and answer to whom something belongs.
- ✓ Can exchange phone numbers with someone.
- ✓ Can express agreement or confirmation.

Model Conversation : ⑧

＜In the Classroom＞

Takahashi ： Budi-san, sore wa nan desu ka.

Budi ： Kore desu ka. Happyoo no shiryoo desu.

Takahashi ： Hee, Budi-san no desu ka.

Budi ： Iie, Min-san no desu.

Takahashi ： Min-san? Donata desu ka.

Budi ： Min-san wa ryoo no tomodachi desu. Betonamu-jin desu.

Takahashi ： Soo desu ka.

Structural Exercises : oral

1

れい) 1. これは つくえです。
2. A：それは なんですか。
B：つくえです。

2

れい) 1. これは わたしの ほんです。
2. A：これは だれの ①ほんですか。
B：②わたしのです。
3. この ほんは わたしのです。

Structural Exercises : oral

1

e.g.) 1. Kore wa <u>tsukue</u> desu.
   2. A : Sore wa nan desu ka.
      B : <u>Tsukue</u> desu.

2

e.g.) 1. Kore wa <u>watashi</u> no hon desu.
   2. A : Kore wa dare no ① <u>hon</u> desu ka.
      B : ② <u>Watashi no</u> desu.
   3. Kono hon wa <u>watashi no</u> desu.

3

れい)　A：それは　なんですか。
　　　　B：これですか。にほんごの　じしょです。

　1)　せんもんの　ほん
　2)　しりょうの　コピー
　3)　にほんごの　きょうかしょ
　4)　コンピューターの　ざっし

4

れい)　A：せんもんは　なんですか。
　　　　B：コンピューターです。

　1)　きょういく
　2)　こくさいかんけい
　3)　かがく

5

れい)　1.　①だいがくの　でんわばんごうは　②0561-74-1111です。
　　　　2.　A：①だいがくの　でんわばんごうは　なんばんですか。
　　　　　　B：②0561-74-1111です。

3

e.g.) A : Sore wa nan desu ka.
　　　B : Kore desu ka. <u>Nihon-go no jisho</u> desu.

1) sen'mon no hon
2) shiryoo no kopii
3) Nihon-go no kyookasho
4) kon'pyuutaa no zasshi

4

e.g.) A : Sen'mon wa nan desu ka.
　　　B : <u>Kon'pyuutaa</u> desu.

1) kyooiku
2) kokusai kan'kee
3) kagaku

5

e.g.) 1. ①<u>Daigaku</u> no den'wa ban'goo wa ②<u>0561-74-1111</u> desu.
　　　2. A : ①<u>Daigaku</u> no den'wa ban'goo wa nan-ban desu ka.
　　　　　B : ②<u>0561-74-1111</u> desu.

Conversational Exercises:

1. ブディ：これ、さとうさんの　じしょですか。
　　　さとう：あ、そうです。どうも　ありがとう。

　　1）ケータイ
　　2）マナカ

2.　ハイン：それは　なんですか。
　　　ブディ：これですか。①コンピューターの②ざっしです。
　　　ハイン：ブディさんのですか。
　　　ブディ：いいえ、③ワンさんのですよ。

　　1）①にほんご　　②しゅくだい　③チンさん
　　2）①はっぴょう　②しりょう　　③まりさん

3.　チン　　　：すみません。
　　　　　　　　　①にっしんだいがくの　でんわばんごうは　なんばんですか。
　　　たかはし：②052-952-7584です。
　　　チン　　　：②052-952-7584ですね。
　　　たかはし：はい、そうです。

　　1）①あおぞらとしょかん　　②0561-73-7111
　　2）①ふじやまえき　　　　　②0561-74-1111

— 26 —

Conversational Exercises :

1. Budi : Kore, Satoo-san no <u>jisho</u> desu ka.
　　Satoo : A, soo desu. Doomo arigatoo.

1) keetai
2) Manaka

2. Hain : Sore wa nan desu ka.
　　Budi : Kore desu ka. ①<u>Kon'pyuutaa</u> no ②<u>zasshi</u> desu.
　　Hain : Budi-san no desu ka.
　　Budi : Iie, ③<u>Wan-san</u> no desu yo.

1) ① Nihon-go　② shukudai　③ Chin-san
2) ① happyoo　② shiryoo　③ Mari-san

3. Chin　　 : Sumimasen.
　　　　　　　①<u>Nisshin Daigaku</u> no den'wa ban'goo wa nan-ban desu ka.
　　Takahashi : ②<u>052-953-7584</u> desu.
　　Chin　　 : ②<u>052-953-7584</u> desu ne.
　　Takahashi : Hai, soo desu.

1) ① Aozora Toshokan　② 0561-73-7111
2) ① Fujiyama Eki　　② 0561-74-1111

— 27 —

Structural Exercices : writing

1. れい)【 これ ・ ほん ・ の ・ です ・ にほんご ・ は 】

→ これは　にほんごの　ほんです。

1)【 は ・ ざっし ・ ぶつり ・ あれ ・ の ・ です 】

→_____

2)【 なん ・ それ ・ か ・ です ・ は 】

→_____

3)【 タンさん ・ じしょ ・ の ・ それ ・ です ・ は 】

→_____

4)【 です ・ アンさん ・ でんわばんごう ・ は ・ の ・ なんばん ・ か 】

→_____

2. れい)【 チンさん ・ だれ 】

A：それは だれ の　ざっしですか。

B： チンさん のです。

1)【 もりさん ・ だれ ・ わたし 】

タイ　　：これは　よしださんの　かさですか。

よしだ：いいえ、_____のじゃ　ありません。

タイ　　：_____の　かさですか。

よしだ：_____のです。

2)【 だれ ・ なん ・ せんもん 】

A：それは_____の　ほんですか。

B：_____の　ほんです。

A：_____のですか。

B：たかはしさんのです。

Structural Exercices : writing

1. e.g.) 【 kore ・ hon ・ no ・ desu ・ Nihon-go ・ wa 】

→ Kore wa Nihon-go no hon desu.

1) 【 wa ・ zasshi ・ butsuri ・ are ・ no ・ desu 】

→ _____

2) 【 nan ・ sore ・ ka ・ desu ・ wa 】

→ _____

3) 【 Tan-san ・ jisho ・ no ・ sore ・ desu ・ wa 】

→ _____

4) 【 desu ・ An-san ・ den'wa ban'goo ・ wa ・ no ・ nan-ban ・ ka 】

→ _____

2. e.g.) 【 Chin-san ・ dare 】

A : Sore wa _dare_ no zasshi desu ka.

B : _Chin-san_ no desu.

1) 【 Mori-san ・ dare ・ watashi 】

Tai   : Kore wa Yoshida-san no kasa desu ka.

Yoshida : Iie, _____ no ja' arimasen.

Tai   : _____ no kasa desu ka.

Yoshida : _____ no desu.

2) 【 dare ・ nan ・ sen'mon 】

A : Sore wa _____ no hon desu ka.

B : _____ no hon desu.

A : _____ no desu ka.

B : Takahashi-san no desu.

— 29 —

3. れい）

れい) A：それは　かがくの__ざっし__ですか。
　　　B：いいえ、__コンピューター__の__ざっし__です。
　　　A：だれのですか。
　　　B：__チンさん__のです。

1) A：それは　コンピューターの　ほんですか。
　　B：いいえ、_____の　ほんです。
　　A：だれのですか。
　　B：_____のです。

2) A：それは　なんですか。
　　B：これですか。_____ の_____です。
　　A：Bさんのですか。
　　B：_____、_____のです。

3) A：それは　なんですか。
　　B：これですか。_____ の _____ です。
　　A：そうですか。

— 30 —

3. e.g.)

e.g.) A : Sore wa kagaku no _zasshi_ desu ka.
　　　B : Iie, _kon'pyuutaa_ no _zasshi_ desu.
　　　A : Dare no desu ka.
　　　B : _Chin-san_ no desu.

1) A : Sore wa kon'pyuutaa no hon desu ka.
　　B : Iie, _____ no hon desu.
　　A : Dare no desu ka.
　　B : _____ no desu.

2) A : Sore wa nan desu ka.
　　B : Kore desu ka. _____ no _____ desu.
　　A : B-san no desu ka.
　　B : _____ , _____ no desu.

3) A : Sore wa nan desu ka.
　　B : Kore desu ka. _____ no _____ desu.
　　A : Soo desu ka.

4. れい) A：これは＿＿なん＿＿ですか。

B：ほんです。

1) A：これは ＿＿＿＿＿＿＿＿＿＿＿＿＿ ほんですか。

B：なかむらせんせいの　ほんです。

2) A：これは ＿＿＿＿＿＿＿＿＿＿＿＿＿ ほんですか。

B：コンピューターの　ほんです。

3) A：だいがくの　でんわばんごうは ＿＿＿＿＿＿＿＿＿＿＿＿ ですか。

B：052-338-1546です。

5. れい) A：これは　なんです（か・ね・よ）。

B：ほんです。

1) A：それは　コンピューターの　ほんですか。

B：はい、そうです。

A：だれのですか。

B：チンさんのです（か・ね・よ）。

2) A：でんわばんごうは　なんばんですか。

B：0561-73-4123です。

A：0561-73-4123です（か・ね・よ）。

B：はい、そうです。

3) A：これ、Bさんのですか。

B：いいえ、Cさんのです。

A：ああ、そうです（か・ね・よ）。

4. e.g.)　A : Kore wa nan desu ka.

　　　　　B : Hon desu.

　1)　A : Kore wa _____ hon desu ka.

　　　B : Nakamura sen'see no hon desu.

　2)　A : Kore wa _____ hon desu ka.

　　　B : Kon'pyuutaa no hon desu.

　3)　A : Daigaku no den'wa ban'goo wa _____ desu ka.

　　　B : 052-338-1546 desu.

5. e.g.)　A : Kore wa nan desu ((ka)・　ne　・　yo).

　　　　　B : Hon desu.

　1)　A : Sore wa kon'pyuutaa no hon desu ka.

　　　B : Hai, soo desu.

　　　A : Dare no desu ka.

　　　B : Chin-san no desu (ka　・　ne　・　yo).

　2)　A : Den'wa ban'goo wa nan-ban desu ka.

　　　B : 0561-73-4123 desu.

　　　A : 0561-73-4123 desu (ka　・　ne　・　yo).

　　　B : Hai, soo desu.

　3)　A : Kore, B-san no desu ka.

　　　B : Iie, C-san no desu.

　　　A : Aa, soo desu (ka　・　ne　・　yo).

Lesson 3

パーティで
At a Party

Targets :
- Can ask or answer questions about how food tastes.
- Can make simple comments about food (e.g. 'This is good.').
- Can ask for comments while sharing a meal with a friend.
- Can ask if someone can eat something (e.g. 'Are you ok with...?') and answer such questions when asked

Model Conversation : ⑫

＜At a Welcome Party＞

さとう	：	さあ、みなさん、どうぞ。
チン	：	わあ、すごいですね。おいしそうですねえ。
アン	：	わあ、おいしそう！
ぜんいん	：	いただきます。

さとう	：	どうですか。おいしいですか。
アン	：	はい、おいしいです。
さとう	：	チンさんは？わさび、からくないですか。
チン	：	はい、だいじょうぶです。
たかはし	：	アンさんは　わさび、だいじょうぶですか。
アン	：	うーん、わたしは　ちょっと・・。わさびは　からすぎます。

Lesson 3

Paatii de
At a Party

Targets:
- Can ask or answer questions about how food tastes.
- Can make simple comments about food (e.g. 'This is good.').
- Can ask for comments while sharing a meal with a friend.
- Can ask if someone can eat something (e.g. 'Are you ok with…?') and answer such questions when asked

Model Conversation : ⑫

< At a Welcome Party >

Satoo	:	Saa, mina-san, doozo.
Chin	:	Waa, sugoi desu ne. Oishisoo desu nee.
An	:	Waa, oishisoo !
Zen'in	:	Itadakimasu.

Satoo	:	Doo desu ka. Oishii desu ka.
An	:	Hai, oishii desu.
Satoo	:	Chin-san wa? Wasabi, karakunai desu ka.
Chin	:	Hai, daijoobu desu.
Takahashi	:	An-san wa wasabi, daijoobu desu ka.
An	:	Uun, watashi wa chotto…. Wasabi wa karasugimasu.

— 35 —

Structural Exercises : oral

1

れい) A: それは なんですか。
　　　 B: <u>おにぎり</u>です。

2

れい) <u>おいしい</u>です。
　　　 <u>おいしくない</u>です。
　　　 <u>おいしかった</u>です。
　　　 <u>おいしくなかった</u>です。

Structural Exercises : oral

1

e.g.) A : Sore wa nan desu ka.

B : <u>Onigiri</u> desu.

2

e.g.) <u>Oishii</u> desu.

<u>Oishikunai</u> desu.

<u>Oishikatta</u> desu.

<u>Oishikunakatta</u> desu.

3

れい) <u>たいへんです。</u>
　　　<u>たいへんじゃ ありません。</u>
　　　<u>たいへんでした。</u>
　　　<u>たいへんじゃ ありませんでした。</u>

4

れい)　A：①<u>にほんごの べんきょう</u>は どうですか。
　　　B：②<u>おもしろい</u>です。

1) ①せんもんの べんきょう　　②いそがしい
2) ①にほんの せいかつ　　　　②たいへん
3) ①にほんの たべもの　　　　②おいしい

5

れい)　A：<u>おいし</u>そうですね。
　　　B：そうですね。

— 38 —

3

e.g.) <u>Taihen desu</u>.

<u>Taihen ja' arimasen</u>.

<u>Taihen deshita</u>.

<u>Taihen ja' arimasen deshita</u>.

4

e.g.) A : ① <u>Nihon-go no ben'kyoo</u> wa doo desu ka.

B : ② <u>Omoshiroi</u> desu.

1) ① sen'mon no ben'kyoo ② isogashii

2) ① Nihon no seekatsu ② taihen

3) ① Nihon no tabemono ② oishii

5

e.g.) A : <u>Oishi</u>soo desu ne.

B : Soo desu ne.

6

れい） <u>たか</u>すぎます。

1） いそがしいです
2） あまいです
3） からいです
4） おおきいです

7

れい） ①<u>にほんの くだものは</u> ②<u>あまい</u>ですが、③<u>たか</u>すぎます。

1） ①せんもんの べんきょう　②おもしろい　　　③いそがしい
2） ①にほんご　　　　　　　②たのしい　　　　③むずかしい

6

e.g.) Takasugi masu.

1) isogashii desu.
2) amai desu.
3) karai desu.
4) ookii desu.

7

e.g.) ① Nihon no kudamono wa ② amai desu ga, ③ takasugimasu.

1) ① sen'mon no ben'kyoo   ② omoshiroi   ③ isogashii
2) ① Nihon-go   ② tanoshii   ③ muzukashii

Conversational Exercises:

1. さとう：<u>からく</u>ないですか。
⑬ ミン　：｛いいえ、だいじょうぶです。
　　　　　｛はい、ちょっと・・・。

　1)　あついです
　2)　あまいです

2. ブディ　　：わあ、①<u>おいしそう</u>ですね。なんですか。
⑭ たかはし：これですか。　②<u>からあげ</u>ですよ。
　ブディ　　：②<u>からあげ</u>ですか。

　1)　①からい　　　②ホットチキン
　2)　①あつい　　　②にくまん

3. もり：①<u>にほんの　たべもの</u>は　どうですか。
⑮ アン：②<u>おいしい</u>です。でも　③<u>わがし</u>は　ちょっと　④<u>あま</u>すぎます。
　もり：そうですか。

　1)　①せんもんの　べんきょう　　　②たのしい
　　　③スケジュール　　　　　　　　④いそがしい
　2)　①にほんごの　べんきょう　　　②おもしろい
　　　③カタカナ　　　　　　　　　　④むずかしい

— 42 —

Conversational Exercises :

1. Satoo : <u>Karaku</u>nai desu ka.
Min : { Iie, daijoobu desu.
        Hai, chotto… .

1) atsui desu
2) amai desu

2. Budi : Waa, ①<u>oishisoo</u> desu ne. Nan desu ka.
Takahashi : Kore desu ka. ②<u>Kara'age</u> desu yo.
Budi : ③ <u>Kara'age</u> desu ka.

1) ① karai   ② hotto chikin
2) ① atsui   ② nikuman

3. Mori : ① <u>Nihon no tabemono</u> wa doo desu ka.
An : ② <u>Oishii</u> desu. Demo ③ <u>wagashi</u> wa chotto ④ <u>ama</u>sugimasu.
Mori : Soo desu ka.

1) ① sen'mon no ben'kyoo   ② tanoshii
   ③ sukejuuru   ④ isogashii
2) ① Nihon-go no ben'kyoo   ② omoshiroi
   ③ katakana   ④ muzukashii

Structural Exercices : writing

1. れい）【 ほん ・ この ・ です ・ おもしろい ・ は 】
　　　　→<u>この　ほん　は　おもしろいです。</u>

1)【 は ・ おいしい ・ からあげ ・ この ・ です 】
　　→ _____

2)【 おおきい ・ かばん ・ は ・ です ・ あの 】
　　→ _____

3)【 どう ・ その ・ か ・ です ・ は ・ ほん 】
　　→ _____

4)【 タンさん ・ です ・ しんせつ ・ は ・ とても 】
　　→ _____

5)【 は ・ とけい ・ たかそうです ・ あの 】
　　→ _____

2. れい）【 チンさん ・ だれ 】
　　　A：それは<u>　だれ　</u>の　ざっしですか。
　　　B：<u>　チンさん　</u>のです。

1)【 むずかしい ・ どう 】
　　タイ　　：よしださん、べんきょうは _____ ですか。
　　よしだ：とても_____です。

2)【 いそがしい ・ たいへん 】
　　チン：アンさん、まいにち _____ ですか。
　　アン：はい、いそがしいです。とても _____ です。

3)【 おいしい ・ おいしそう 】
　　ミン　　　：わあ、これ _____ ですね。
　　たかはし：とても _____ ですよ。どうぞ。

4)【 どうぞ ・ どう 】
　　よしだ　：これ、_____ 。
　　アン　　：わあ、いただきます。
　　よしだ　：_____ ですか。
　　アン　　：おいしいですね。

— 44 —

Structural Exercices : writing

1. e.g.) 【 hon ・ kono ・ desu ・ omoshiroi ・ wa 】

→ Kono hon wa omoshiroi desu.

1) 【 wa ・ oishii ・ kara'age ・ kono ・ desu 】

→_____

2) 【 ookii ・ kaban ・ wa ・ desu ・ ano 】

→_____

3) 【 doo ・ sono ・ ka ・ desu ・ wa ・ hon 】

→_____

4) 【 Tan-san ・ desu ・ shin'setsu ・ wa ・ totemo 】

→_____

5) 【 wa ・ tokee ・ takasoo desu ・ ano 】

→_____

2. e.g.) 【 Chin-san ・ dare 】

A : Sore wa _dare_ no zasshi desu ka.

B : _Chin-san_ no desu.

1) 【 muzukashii ・ doo 】

Tai　　　: Yoshida-san, ben'kyoo wa _____ desu ka.

Yoshida : Totemo _____ desu.

2) 【 isogashii ・ taihen 】

Chin : An-san, mai-nichi _____ desu ka.

An　 : Hai, isogashii desu. Totemo _____ desu.

3) 【 oishii ・ oishisoo 】

Min　　　 : Waa, kore _____ desu ne.

Takahashi : Totemo _____ desu yo. Doozo.

4) 【 doozo ・ doo 】

Yoshida : Kore, _____ .

An　　　 : Waa, itadakimasu.

Yoshida : _____ desu ka.

An　　　 : Oishii desu ne.

— 45 —

3. れい) A：これは　ほんですか。【はい】
　　　　 B：　はい、ほんです。

1) A：その　ほんは　おもしろいですか。【はい】
　　 B：＿＿＿＿＿＿＿＿＿＿＿＿＿＿＿＿＿＿＿＿＿＿＿＿＿＿＿＿。

2) A：それは、からいですか。【いいえ】
　　 B：＿＿＿＿＿＿＿＿＿＿＿＿＿＿＿＿＿＿＿＿＿＿＿＿＿＿＿＿。

3) A：Bさん、だいじょうぶですか。【はい】
　　 B：＿＿＿＿＿＿＿＿＿＿＿＿＿＿＿＿＿＿＿＿＿＿＿＿＿＿＿＿。

4. れい) A：これは　＿なん＿　ですか。
　　　　 B：ほんです。

1) A：にほんごの　べんきょうは ＿＿＿＿＿＿＿＿＿＿＿＿＿ ですか。
　　 B：おもしろいです。

2) A：せんせいは ＿＿＿＿＿＿＿＿＿＿＿＿＿ ですか。
　　 B：はい、とても　しんせつです。

3) A：これは ＿＿＿＿＿＿＿＿＿＿＿＿＿ ですか。
　　 B：からあげです。
　　 A：からあげは ＿＿＿＿＿＿＿＿＿＿＿＿＿ ですか。
　　 B：おいしいです。

3. e.g.) A : Kore wa hon desu ka. 【 Hai 】

B :   Hai, hon desu.

1) A : Sono hon wa omoshiroi desu ka. 【 Hai 】

   B : _____ .

2) A : Sore wa, karai desu ka. 【 Iie 】

   B : _____ .

3) A : B-san, daijoobu desu ka. 【 Hai 】

   B : _____ .

4. e.g.) A : Kore wa nan desu ka.

B : Hon desu.

1) A : Nihon-go no ben'kyoo wa _____ desu ka.

   B : Omoshiroi desu.

2) A : Sen'see wa _____ desu ka.

   B : Hai, totemo shin'setsu desu.

3) A : Kore wa _____ desu ka.

   B : Kara'age desu.

   A : Kara'age wa _____ desu ka.

   B : Oishii desu.

Lesson 4

みせで
At a Shop

Targets :
- ✓ Can order food or drink with simple expressions such as "this please" while pointing to a picture on a menu at a restaurant.
- ✓ Can ask a person to do shopping for speaker or accept such request when asked.
- ✓ Can ask a price or answer when asked.

Model Conversation : ⑯

＜In a Hamburger Shop＞

おみせのひと ： いらっしゃいませ。ごちゅうもんは？
さとう   ： チーズバーガーと　コーラ、おねがいします。
もり   ： ぼくは　テリヤキバーガー、ふたつ　ください。
おみせのひと ： はい、チーズバーガーと　コーラと　テリヤキバーガー　ふたつ
          ですね。ぜんぶで　1200えんです。
さとう   ： はい。

おみせのひと ： あの、これ、おきゃくさまの　かさですか。
さとう   ： えっ！？　わたしのじゃ　ありません。
          あ、もりさん、もりさんの　ですか。
もり   ： あ、そうです。ありがとう。

Lesson 4

Mise de
At a Shop

> **Targets :**
> ✓ Can order food or drink with simple expressions such as "this please" while pointing to a picture on a menu at a restaurant.
> ✓ Can ask a person to do shopping for speaker or accept such request when asked.
> ✓ Can ask a price or answer when asked.

Model Conversation : ⑯

＜In a Hamburger Shop＞

O-mise no hito	：	Irasshaimase. Go-chuumon wa?
Satoo	：	Chiizu-baagaa to koora, onegaishimasu.
Mori	：	Boku wa teriyaki-baagaa, futatsu kudasai.
O-mise no hito	：	Hai, chiizu-baagaa to koora to teriyaki-baagaa futatsu desu ne. Zen'bu de 1200-en desu.
Satoo	：	Hai.

O-mise no hito	：	Ano, kore, o-kyaku-sama no kasa desu ka.
Satoo	：	Eh!? Watashi no ja' arimasen. A, Mori-san, Mori-san no desu ka.
Mori	：	A, soo desu. Arigatoo.

— 49 —

Structural Exercises : oral

1

いくつですか。

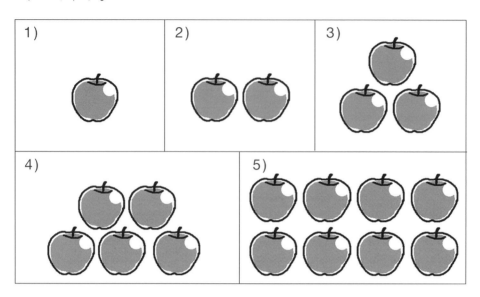

2

れい) A：いくらですか。
　　　B：500えんです。

1) 600　　2) 980　　3) 370　　4) 8,300

3

れい) A：すみません、いくらですか。
　　　B：15,000えんです。
　　　A：15,000えんですね。
　　　B：はい。

1) 7,800　　2) 74,600　　3) 38,000　　4) 143,000

Structural Exercises : oral

1

Ikutsu desu ka.

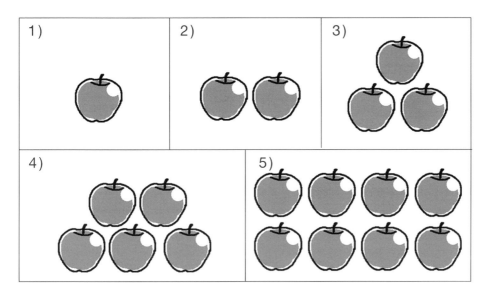

2

e.g.) A : Ikura desu ka.
       B : <u>500</u>-en desu.

1) 600   2) 980   3) 370   4) 8,300

3

e.g.) A : Sumimasen, ikura desu ka.
       B : <u>15,000</u>-en desu.
       A : <u>15,000</u>-en desu ne.
       B : Hai.

1) 7,800   2) 74,600   3) 38,000   4) 143,000

4

れい）　コーヒーと　サンドイッチ、おねがいします。

5

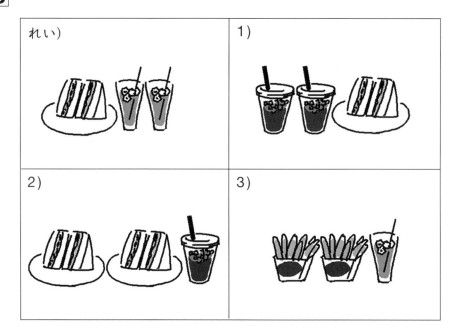

れい）　サンドイッチと　ジュース　ふたつ、おねがいします。

4

e.g.) <u>Koohii to san'doicchi,</u> onegaishimasu.

5

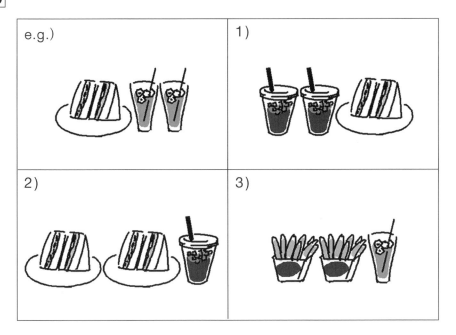

e.g.) <u>San'doicchi to juusu futatsu,</u> onegaishimasu.

Conversational Exercises :

1. Satoo-san is going to a convenience store.
⑰
さとう　：わたし、コンビニ、いってきます。
ミン　　：あ、いっしょに　①コーラ　｛おねがいできますか。
　　　　　　　　　　　　　　　　　　　いいですか。
さとう　：いいですよ。
アン　　：じゃ、わたしも　②コーヒー、おねがいします。
さとう　：はい。

さとう　：ただいま。
ミン　　：あ、ありがとう。いくらですか。
さとう　：③200えんです。
アン　　：わたしは？
さとう　：④150えんです。
アン　　：はい、ありがとう。

1)　①おにぎり　ふたつ　　　　②カップラーメン　ひとつ
　　③250えん　　　　　　　　　④130えん
2)　①フライドチキン　ひとつ　②にくまん　ふたつ
　　③200えん　　　　　　　　　④300えん

2.　ブディ　　　：すみません、①コーヒー、ふたつ　おねがいします。
⑱　　みせのひと：①コーヒー、ふたつですね。かしこまりました。

　　1)　①ハンバーガー　みっつ
　　2)　①コーヒーと　サンドイッチ

3.　ミン　：その①パソコン、②いいですね。
⑲　　ハイン：ええ、とても　べんりです。
　　ミン　：いくらですか。
　　ハイン：えーっと、③150,000えんぐらいでした。
　　ミン　：そうですか。いいですね。

　　1)　① iPad　　　　　②あたらしい　　　③50,000えん
　　2)　①でんしじしょ　②べんりそう　　　③20,000えん

Conversational Exercises :

1. Satoo-san is going to a convenience store.
⑰
Satoo ：Watashi, kon'bini, ittekimasu.
Minh ：A, issho ni ①koora ┌onegai dekimasu ka.
　　　　　　　　　　　　　└ii desu ka.
Satoo ：Ii desu yo.
An ：Ja, watashi mo ②koohii, onegaishimasu.
Satoo ：Hai.

Satoo ：Tadaima.
Minh ：A, arigatoo. Ikura desu ka.
Satoo ：③200-en desu.
An ：Watashi wa?
Satoo ：④150-en desu.
An ：Hai, arigatoo.

1) ① onigiri futatsu　　　② kappu raamen hitotsu
　　③ 250-en　　　　　　④ 130-en
2) ① furaido chikin hitotsu　② nikuman futatsu
　　③ 200-en　　　　　　④ 300-en

2.　Budi　　　　：Sumimasen, <u>koohii, futatsu</u> onegaishimasu.
⑱　Mise no hito ：<u>Koohii, futatsu</u> desu ne. Kashikomarimashita.

　　1) han'baagaa mittsu
　　2) koohii to san'doicchi

3.　Minh ：Sono ①pasokon, ②Ii desu ne.
⑲　Hain ：Ee, totemo ben'ri desu.
　　Minh ：Ikura desu ka.
　　Hain ：Eeto, ③150,000-en gurai deshita.
　　Minh ：Soo desu ka. Ii desu ne.

　　1) ① iPad　　　　② atarashii　　　③ 50,000-en
　　2) ① den'shi jisho　② ben'risoo　　　③ 20,000-en

Structural Exercices : writing

1.

1	ひとつ	2		3		4		5	
6		7		8		9		10	

2.

100	ひゃく	200		300	
600		800		1,000	
3,000		8,000		10,000	
6,400		89,700			

3. 1) 【 みっつ ・ おねがいします ・ チーズバーガー 】

　　→_____

　2) 【 コーヒー ・ おねがいします ・ サンドイッチ ・ と 】

　　→_____

　3) 【 ぜんぶ ・ いくらです ・ で ・ か 】

　　→_____

Structural Exercices : writing

1.

1	hitotsu	2		3		4		5	
6		7		8		9		10	

2.

100	hyaku	200		300	
600		800		1,000	
3,000		8,000		10,000	
6,400		89,700			

3. 1) 【 mittsu ・ onegaishimasu ・ chiizu-baagaa 】

→ _____

2) 【 koohii ・ onegaishimasu ・ san'doicchi ・ to 】

→ _____

3) 【 zen'bu ・ ikura desu ・ de ・ ka 】

→ _____

4 みせで / Mise de / At a Shop

4. 1)　【400えん ・ ふたつ ・ ぜんぶ ・ ばいてん ・ いくら】

　　　A： ＿＿＿＿＿＿＿＿＿＿＿ 、　いってきます。

　　　B： あ、いっしょに　サンドイッチ ＿＿＿＿＿＿＿＿＿＿＿ 、いいですか？

　　　A： いいですよ。

　　　＊＊＊＊＊＊＊＊＊＊＊＊＊＊＊＊＊＊＊＊＊＊＊＊＊＊＊＊＊＊＊

　　　A： ただいま。はい、どうぞ。

　　　B： ありがとうございます。＿＿＿＿＿＿＿＿＿＿＿ ですか？

　　　A： ＿＿＿＿＿＿＿＿＿＿＿ で ＿＿＿＿＿＿＿＿＿＿＿ です。

　　2)　【ありがとう ・ Cさん ・ あの ・ えっ】

　　　A： ＿＿＿＿＿＿＿＿＿＿＿ 、これ、Bさんの　かさですか。

　　　B： ＿＿＿＿＿＿＿＿＿＿＿ 、わたしのじゃ　ありません。
　　　　　＿＿＿＿＿＿＿＿＿＿＿ のですか。

　　　C： はい、わたしのです。＿＿＿＿＿＿＿＿＿＿＿ 。

4. 1) 【 400-en ・ futatsu ・ zen'bu ・ baiten ・ ikura 】

A : _____ , ittekimasu.

B : A, issho ni san'doicchi _____ , ii desu ka?

A : Ii desu yo.

****

A : Tadaima. Hai, doozo.

B : Arigatoo gozaimasu. _____ desu ka?

A : _____ de _____ desu.

2) 【 arigatoo ・ C-san ・ ano ・ eh 】

A : _____ , kore, B-san no kasa desu ka.

B : _____ , watashi no ja' arimasen.

_____ no desu ka.?

A : Hai, watashi no desu. _____ .

— 59 —

Lesson 5

テスト
Exam

Targets:
✓ Can ask the time and place of something and answer such questions when asked.
✓ Can provide simple information on an item and understand such information when given.
✓ Can read and understand a short, simple note written on a message board.

Model Conversation: ⑳

アン： すみません。あしたの テストは なんじからですか。
もり： 1じからです。12じはんに きてください。
　　　ばしょは 205です。
アン： わかりました。205は どこですか。
もり： 2かいですよ。
アン： 2かいですね。ありがとうございます。

せんせい： じゃ、テストを おわりましょう。
アン　　： つかれましたね。
　　　　　あの、みなさん、これ、どうぞ。
さとう　： えっ！？ なんですか。
アン　　： タイの おかしです。
さとう　： わあ、ありがとうございます。
もり　　： ありがとうございます。
　　　　　いただきます。

Lesson 5

Tesuto
Exam

Targets:
✓ Can ask the time and place of something and answer such questions when asked.
✓ Can provide simple information on an item and understand such information when given.
✓ Can read and understand a short, simple note written on a message board.

Model Conversation : ⑳

An	:	Sumimasen. Ashita no tesuto wa nan-ji kara desu ka.
Mori	:	1-ji kara desu. 12-ji han ni kite kudasai.
		Basho wa 205 desu.
An	:	Wakarimashita. 205 wa doko desu ka.
Mori	:	2-kai desu yo.
An	:	2-kai desu ne. Arigatoo gozaimasu.

Sen'see	:	Ja, tesuto o owarimashoo.
An	:	Tsukaremashita ne.
		Ano, mina-san, kore, doozo.
Satoo	:	Eh!? Nan desu ka.
An	:	Tai no o-kashi desu.
Satoo	:	Waa, arigatoo gozaimasu.
Mori	:	Arigatoo gozaimasu. Itadakimasu.

Structural Exercises : oral

1

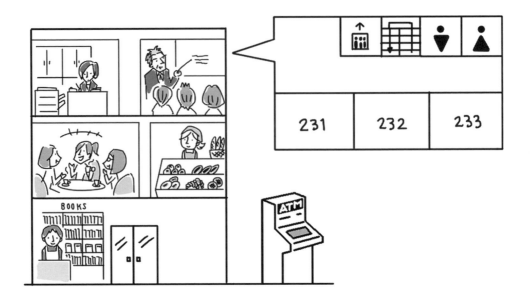

れい）1. A：すみません、①トイレは　どこですか。
　　　　B：②あそこです。
　　　　A：どうも。

　　　2. A：すみません、①ほんやは　どこですか。
　　　　B：②1かいです。
　　　　A：どうも。

2

1) おなまえは？

2) おくには　どちらですか。

1) ＿＿＿＿＿＿＿＿＿＿＿＿＿＿＿
2) ＿＿＿＿＿＿＿＿＿＿＿＿＿＿＿

SURVIVAL JAPANESE

FOR UNIVERSITY STUDENTS
1

ごい・ひょうげん

Vocabularies / Expressions

SOBI-SHUPPANSHA

Useful Expressions
Aisatsu - Greetings

Japanese	Pronunciation	English
なまえ	namae	name
しゅくだい	shukudai	homework
しつもん	shitsumon	question
こたえ	kotae	answer
れい	ree	example
はじめましょう	hajimemashoo	Let's start.
おわりましょう	owarimashoo	Let's finish.
やすみましょう	yasumimashoo	Let's take a break.
わかりますか	wakarimasu ka	Do you understand?
わかりました	wakarimashita	I understand.
わかりません	wakarimasen	I don't understand.
いって ください	itte kudasai	Please say.
かいて ください	kaite kudasai	Please write.
きいて ください	kiite kudasai	Please listen.
きて ください	kite kudasai	Please come.
みて ください	mite kudasai	Please look.
よんで ください	yon'de kudasai	Please read.
～して ください	～shite kudasai	Please do (something).
いいです	ii desu	That's fine. / That's good.
ちがいます	chigaimasu	That's wrong.
もういちど	moo ichido	once more
おはようございます	ohayoo gozaimasu	Good morning.
こんにちは	kon'nichiwa	Hello. / Good afternoon.
こんばんは	kon'banwa	Good evening.
さようなら	sayoonara	Good bye.
ありがとうございます	arigatoo gozaimasu	Thank you.
おねがいします	onegai shimasu	Please.
しつれいします	shitsuree shimasu	Please excuse me. / I must be off. (used when leaving)
じゃ、また	ja, mata	See you.
すみません	sumimasen	I'm sorry. / Excuse me.

Lesson 1 Jiko Shookai – Self-Introduction

Japanese	Pronunciation	English
がくせい	gakusee	student
りゅうがくせい	ryuugakusee	international student
こうかんりゅうがくせい	kookan ryuugakusee	international exchange student
だいがくいんせい	daigakuin'see	graduate student
いんせい	in'see	graduate student (short form)
けんきゅういん	ken'kyuuin	researcher
けんきゅうせい	ken'kyuusee	research student
ここの　がくせい	koko no gakusee	student of this university / institution
じむの　ひと	jimu no hito	office staff
せんせい	sen'see	teacher / instructor (not used when referring to one's own job) / suffix added to a name of teacher
じょしゅ	joshu	teaching assistant (TA)
せんぱい	sen'pai	senior (a student who has studied longer than you)
ドクター	dokutaa	doctor's (Ph.D.)
マスター	masutaa	master's (degree)
わたし / ぼく	watashi / boku	I
あの　ひと(あの　かた)	ano hito (ano kata)	that person / he / she （あの　かた [ano-kata] is the polite equivalent of あの　ひと [ano-hito]）
〜さん	〜san	Mr. / Ms. (suffix added to a name for expressing politeness)
〜じん	〜jin	(suffix 'a national of...' e.g. アメリカじん [amerika-jin] = an American)
だれ(どなた)	dare (donata)	who (どなた [donata] is the polite equivalent of だれ [dare])
せんもん	sen'mon	major
かがく	kagaku	chemistry
きょういく	kyooiku	education
けいざい	keezai	economics
こくさいかんけい	kokusai kan'kee	international relations
ぶつり	butsuri	physics
ほうがく	hoogaku	law
コンピューター	kon'pyuutaa	computer
にほん	nihon	Japan
かんこく	kan'koku	South Korea

—2—

Japanese	Pronunciation	English
ちゅうごく	chuugoku	China
タイ	tai	Thailand
ベトナム	betonamu	Vietnam
マレーシア	mareeshia	Malaysia
だいがく	daigaku	university
あおぞらだいがく	aozora daigaku	Aozora University
にっしんだいがく	nisshin daigaku	Nisshin University
にっしんだい	nisshin dai	Nisshin Uni
Expressions:		
はい	hai	yes
いいえ	iie	no
そう	soo	so / correct
～から きました	～kara kimashita	I'm from (country).
[どうぞ] よろしく	[doozo] yoroshiku	Pleased to meet you. (Lit. 'Please be nice to me.'
[おねがいします]	[onegai shimasu]	Usually used at the end of a self-introduction.)
こちらこそ よろしく	kochirakoso yoroshiku	It's nice to meet yoo too.
おねがいします	onegai shimasu	
しつれいですが…	shitsuree desu ga...	Excuse me, but… (used when asking someone for personal information such as their name or address)
そうですか	soo desu ka	I see.
あ	a	Oh! (used when you realise something)
あの	ano	Well… (used to show hesitation)
こちらは～さんです	kochira wa～san desu	This is Mr. / Ms. (someone) (used when introducing someone politely)
はじめまして	hajimemashite	Nice to meet you. (Lit. 'I am meeting you for the first time.' Usually used as the first phrase when introducing oneself.)
これから いっしょに けんきゅう します	korekara issho ni ken'kyuu shimasu	We'll be researching together.

— 3 —

Lesson 2 Kyooshitsu de (1) – In the Classroom (1)

Japanese	Pronunciation	English
CD	shiidii	CD / compact disk
いす	isu	chair
えんぴつ	en'pitsu	pencil
かぎ	kagi	key
かさ	kasa	umbrella
かばん	kaban	bag / briefcase
きょうかしょ	kyookasho	textbook
ざっし	zasshi	magazine
じしょ	jisho	dictionary
でんしじしょ	den'shi jisho	electronic dictionary
しんぶん	shin'bun	newspaper
ほん	hon	book
つくえ	tsukue	desk
でんわ	den'wa	telephone / phone
とけい	tokee	watch / clock
ケータイ	keetai	mobile phone
スマホ	sumaho	smartphone
シャープペンシル	shaapu pen'shiru	mechanical pencil
ボールペン	boorupen	ballpoint pen
ノート	nooto	notebook
パソコン	pasokon	personal computer
マナカ	manaka	Manaka (IC card for a public transportion in central Japan)
けんきゅう	ken'kyuu	research
しりょう	shiryoo	research materials / data
すうがく	suugaku	mathematics
はっぴょう	happyoo	presentation
ゼミ	zemi	seminar / small class where students do research on the same topic
コピー	kopii	(photo)copy
レジュメ	rejume	summary / outline
レポート	repooto	report
えいご	ee-go	English (language)
にほんご	nihon-go	Japanese (language)
〜ご	〜go	… language (suffix)

— 4 —

Japanese	Pronunciation	English
ともだち	tomodachi	friend
でんわばんごう	den'wa ban'goo	telephone number
りょう	ryoo	dormitory
あおぞらとしょかん	aozora toshokan	Aozora Library
ふじやまえき	fujiyama eki	Fujiyama Station
これ	kore	this thing here
それ	sore	that thing near the listener
あれ	are	that thing over there
この〜	kono〜	this… / this… here
その〜	sono〜	that… / that… near the listener
あの〜	ano〜	that… / that… over there
いち	ichi	one
に	ni	two
さん	san	three
よん／し	yon / shi	four
ご	go	five
ろく	roku	six
なな／しち	nana /shichi	seven
はち	hachi	eight
きゅう／く	kyuu / ku	nine
じゅう	juu	ten
なん	nan	what
なんばん	nan-ban	which number / what number
Expressions:		
ああ	aa	ah, oh
どうも　ありがとう	doomo arigatoo	Thank you.
へえ	hee	Oh, really?

— 5 —

Lesson 3 Paatii de – At a Party

Japanese	Pronunciation	English
［お］すし	[o] sushi	sushi
おにぎり	onigiri	rice ball
からあげ	kara'age	deep fried chicken (Japanese style)
ぎゅうどん	gyuudon	beef bowl
にくまん	nikuman	steamed bun with pork filling
みそしる	misoshiru	miso soup
わがし	wagashi	Japanese sweets
わさび	wasabi	wasabi
たべもの	tabemono	food
ケーキ	keeki	cake
フライドチキン	furaido chikin	deep fried chicken (western style)
ホットチキン	hotto chikin	spicy chicken
せいかつ	seekatsu	life / lifestyle
ひらがな	hiragana	hiragana
カタカナ	katakana	katakana
べんきょう	ben'kyoo	study
スケジュール	sukejuuru	schedule
チケット	chiketto	ticket
パーティー	paatii	party
かんげい　パーティ	kan'gee paatii	welcome party
ぜんいん	zen'in	all members
みなさん	mina-san	everyone (excluding the speaker oneself)
いい	ii	good
いそがしい	isogashii	busy
あつい	atsui	hot
つめたい	tsumetai	cold (to touch)
あまい	amai	sweet
おいしい	oishii	delicious
おおきい	ookii	big / large
ちいさい	chiisai	small / little
おもしろい	omoshiroi	interesting / funny
からい	karai	hot / spicy

— 6 —

Japanese	Pronunciation	English
すごい	sugoi	amazing / awesome
たかい	takai	expensive
やすい	yasui	cheap
たのしい	tanoshii	fun / enjoyable
むずかしい	muzukashii	difficult
かんたん	kan'tan	easy / simple
しんせつ	shin'setsu	helpful / kind
だいじょうぶ	daijoobu	all right / fine
たいへん	taihen	tough (sometimes used to mean 'extremely')
ひま	hima	free (time)
まいにち	mainichi	everyday
どう	doo	how
あまり	amari	not so / not so much (used with negatives)
ちょっと	chotto	a little / a little while
とても	totemo	very

Expressions:

Japanese	Pronunciation	English
さあ	saa	go on / all right (used when encouraging someone to do something)
どうぞ	doozo	Here you are. (used when offering someone something)
わあ！	waa!	Wow! (used for pleasant surprises or admiration)
いただきます	itadakimasu	Let's eat. (Lit. 'I partake.' Used before meals.)
うーん	uun	Umm… (used when thinking)
ちょっと・・・	chotto…	Well… (softens whatever is said afterwards)

Lesson 4 Mise de – At a Shop

Japanese	Pronunciation	English
カップラーメン	kappu raamen	cup noodle
サンドイッチ	san'doicchi	sandwich
チーズバーガー	chiizu baagaa	cheese burger
テリヤキバーガー	teriyaki baagaa	teriyaki burger
ハンバーガー	han'baagaa	hamburger
アイスティー	aisu tii	iced tea
カフェラテ	kafe rate	cafe latte
コーヒー	koohii	coffee
アイスコーヒー	aisu koohii	iced coffee
コーラ	koora	cola
ジュース	juusu	juice
おちゃ	o-cha	tea
あたらしい	atarashii	new / fresh
ふるい	furui	old
べんり	ben'ri	convenient
コンビニ	kon'bini	convenience store
せいきょう	seekyoo	Co-op store
ばいてん	baiten	stand / campus store
ひゃく	hyaku	one hundred
せん	sen	one thousand
まん	man	ten thousand
ひとつ	hitotsu	one (quantifier for counting apples, erasers, chairs, etc.)
ふたつ	futatsu	two (quantifier for counting apples, erasers, chairs, etc.)
みっつ	mittsu	three (quantifier for counting apples, erasers, chairs, etc.)
よっつ	yottsu	four (quantifier for counting apples, erasers, chairs, etc.)
いつつ	itsutsu	five (quantifier for counting apples, erasers, chairs, etc.)
むっつ	muttsu	six (quantifier for counting apples, erasers, chairs, etc.)
ななつ	nanatsu	seven (quantifier for counting apples, erasers, chairs, etc.)
やっつ	yattsu	eight (quantifier for counting apples, erasers, chairs, etc.)
ここのつ	kokonotsu	nine (quantifier for counting apples, erasers, chairs, etc.)
とお	too	ten (quantifier for counting apples, erasers, chairs, etc.)

Japanese	Pronunciation	English
〜えん	〜en	(amount) yen (suffix)
いくつ	ikutsu	how many
いくら	ikura	how much
くらい（ぐらい）	kurai [gurai]	around / approx.
ぜんぶで	zen'bu de	in total
Expressions:		
いってきます	ittekimasu	I'm off. (used when you leave, intending to return)
いっしょに	issho ni	Can I ask you (something) all together?
おねがいできますか	onegai dekimasu ka	
いいですか	ii desu ka	Is it OK?
ただいま	tadaima	I'm back. / I'm home. (used when you return somewhere)
じゃ	ja	well / then / in that case
えーっと	eetto	Uhh… (used when you are thinking of what to say)
ええ	ee	Yes.
かしこまりました	kashikomarimashita	Certainly. / Sure. (very polire)
おみせの　ひと	o-mise no hito	shop assisstant / shop clark
おきゃくさま	o-kyaku-sama	customer
いらっしゃいませ	irasshaimase	Welcome. / May I help you? (a greeting to a customer or a guest entering a shop, etc.)
ごちゅうもんは？	go-chuumon wa?	May I take your order?
〜、おねがいします	〜, onegai shimasu	(one's order), please.
〜、ください	〜, kudasai	Give me (one's order).
えっ!?	e!?	What!? (used when hearing something unexpected)

— 9 —

Lesson 5 Tesuto – Exam

Japanese	Pronunciation	English
Vocabulary:		
おきます	okimasu	to wake up
ねます	nemasu	to sleep / to go to bed
はじまります	hajimarimasu	to begin / to start
おわります	owarimasu	to finish / to end
べんきょうします	benkyoo shimasu	to study
はやい	hayai	fast / early
おそい	osoi	slow / late
ここ	koko	here / this place
そこ	soko	there / that place (near the listener)
あそこ	asoko	(that place) over there
こちら	kochira	this way / this place (polite equivalent of ここ [koko])
そちら	sochira	that way / that place (near the listener) (polite equivalent of そこ [soko])
あちら	achira	that way / the place over there (polite equivalent of あそこ [asoko])
どこ	doko	where
どちら	dochira	which way / where (polite equivalent of どこ [doko])
ばしょ	basho	place
［お］くに	[o] kuni	(your) country
うち	uchi	house / home
へや	heya	room
ATM	eetiiemu	ATM
ぎんこう	gin'koo	bank
としょかん	toshokan	library
ゆうびんきょく	yuubin'kyoku	post office
ビル（たてもの）	biru (tatemono)	building
カフェ	kafe	café
パンや	pan-ya	bakery
ほんや	hon-ya	book store
デパート	depaato	department store
かいぎしつ	kaigi-shitsu	conference room / meeting room

Japanese	Pronunciation	English
きょうしつ	kyooshitsu	classroom
じっけんしつ	jikkenshitsu	laboratory
しょくどう	shokudoo	dining hall / cafeteria / canteen
じむしつ	jimushitsu	administrative office
かいだん	kaidan	staircase
ちか	chika	basement
じどうはんばいき	jidoo han'baiki	vending machine
エスカレーター	esukareetaa	escalator
エレベーター	erebeetaa	elevator
トイレ(おてあらい)	toire (o-tearai)	toilet / rest room
ロビー	robii	lobby
〜かい(がい)	〜kai (gai)	-th floor
なんがい	nan-gai	which floor
おおさか	oosaka	Osaka
ほっかいどう	hokkaidoo	Hokkaido
きょう	kyoo	today
あした	ashita	tomorrow
きのう	kinoo	yesterday
あさって	asatte	the day after tomorrow
おととい	ototoi	the day before yesterday
げつようび	getsu-yoobi	Monday
かようび	ka-yoobi	Tuesday
すいようび	sui-yoobi	Wednesday
もくようび	moku-yoobi	Thursday
きんようび	kin-yoobi	Friday
どようび	do-yoobi	Saturday
にちようび	nichi-yoobi	Sunday
なんようび	nan-yoobi	which day of the week
やすみ	yasumi	day off / holiday / vacation
ごぜん	gozen	am
ごご	gogo	pm

Japanese	Pronunciation	English
1 じ	ichi-ji	one o'clock
2 じ	ni-ji	two o'clock
3 じ	san-ji	three o'clock
4 じ	yo-ji	four o'clock
5 じ	go-ji	five o'clock
6 じ	roku-ji	six o'clock
7 じ	shichi-ji	seven o'clock
8 じ	hachi-ji	eight o'clock
9 じ	ku-ji	nine o'clock
10 じ	juu-ji	ten o'clock
11 じ	juuichi-ji	eleven o'clock
12 じ	juuni-ji	twelve o'clock
5 ふん	go-fun	5 minutes
10 ぷん	ji-ppun / ju-ppun	10 minutes
はん	han	half hour
なんじ	nan-ji	what time
なんぷん	nan-pun	how many minutes
いま	ima	now
もう	moo	already
まだ	mada	not yet
うちあわせ	uchiawase	meeting to make an arrangement
かいぎ	kaigi	meeting / conference
じゅぎょう	jugyoo	class / lesson
こうぎ	koogi	lecture
じっけん	jikken	experiment
じっしゅう	jisshuu	practicum / practical component
クラス	kurasu	class
メモ	memo	memo
おかし	o-kashi	sweets
おみやげ	o-miyage	souvenir
にんぎょう	nin'gyoo	doll
Tシャツ	T-shatsu	T-shirt
キャンディー	kyan'dii	candy
クッキー	kukkii	cookie
チョコレート	chokoreeto	chocolate

Japanese	Pronunciation	English
Expressions:		
おなまえは？	o-namae wa?	May I have your name?
きて ください	kite kudasai	Please come.
がんばって　ください	gan'batte kudasai	Do your best! / Hang in there! (used to encourage someone facing difficulty)
なんて かいて ありますか	nan'te kaite arimasu ka	What is written? / What does this say?
どうも	doomo	Thanks. (abbreviation of どうもありがとう [doomo arigatoo] / どうもありがとうございました [doomo arigatoogozaimashita])
つかれました	tsukaremashita	I'm tired.
そして	soshite	and then
いただきます	itadakimasu	to receive (humble form of "morau")
さしあげます	sashiagemasu	to give (humble form of "ageru")

Lesson 6 Happyoo – Presentation

Japanese	Pronunciation	English
いきます	ikimasu	to go
かえります	kaerimasu	to return (home)
きます	kimasu	to come
けんきゅうします	ken'kyuu shimasu	to research
じっけんします	jikken shimasu	to do an experiment
じゅんびします	jun'bi shimasu	to prepare
スピーチします	supiichi shimasu	to make a speech / to give a speech
てつやします	tetsuya shimasu	to stay up all night
はたらきます	hatarakimasu	to work
はっぴょうします	happyoo shimasu	to make a presentation
やすみます	yasumimasu	to rest
がんばります	gan'barimasu	to hold out / to do one's best
きょねん	kyo-nen	last year
ことし	kotoshi	this year
らいねん	rai-nen	next year
せんげつ	sen-getsu	last month
こんげつ	kon-getsu	this month
らいげつ	rai-getsu	next month
せんしゅう	sen-shuu	last week
こんしゅう	kon-shuu	this week
らいしゅう	rai-shuu	next week
あさ	asa	morning
ひる	hiru	noon
ばん	ban	evening
まいあさ	mai-asa	every morning
まいばん	mai-ban	every night
けさ	kesa	this morning
こんばん	kon-ban	tonight
ひるやすみ	hiru-yasumi	lunch break
ついたち	tsuitachi	the first (day of the month)
ふつか	futsuka	the second (day of the month)
みっか	mikka	the third (day of the month)

Japanese	Pronunciation	English
よっか	yokka	the forth (day of the month)
いつか	itsuka	the fifth (day of the month)
むいか	muika	the sixth (day of the month)
なのか	nanoka	the seventh (day of the month)
ようか	yooka	the eighth (day of the month)
ここのか	kokonoka	the ninth (day of the month)
とおか	tooka	the tenth (day of the month)
じゅうよっか	juuyokka	the fourteenth (day of the month)
はつか	hatsuka	the twentieth (day of the month)
にじゅうよっか	nijuuyokka	the twenty-fourth (day of the month)
～ねん	～nen	-th year
～から	～kara	from
～まで	～made	to / until
いつ	itsu	when
なんがつ	nan-gatsu	which month
なんにち	nan-nichi	what day of the month / what is the date
なんじに	nan-ji ni	at what time
みんな	min'na	everyone
きょうと	kyooto	Kyoto
おおす	oosu	Osu (the name of a shopping district in downtown Nagoya)
さかえ	sakae	Sakae (the name of shopping district in downtown Nagoya)
ふじさん	fuji-san	Mt. Fuji
がっかい	gakkai	academic conference
けんきゅうかい	ken'kyuu-kai	research society / seminar
けんきゅうしつ	ken'kyuu-shitsu	professor's office
けんしゅうりょこう	ken'shuu ryokoo	study excursion / field trip
いざかや	izakaya	Japanese style pub
カラオケ	karaoke	karaoke
２ごうかん	nigoo-kan	building 2
～かん	～kan	～building (counter for large buildings)

Japanese	Pronunciation	English
ちゅうがっこう	chuugakkoo	junior high school
スーパー	suupaa	supermarket
レストラン	resutoran	restaurant
あるいて	aruite	on foot
くるま	kuruma	car
じてんしゃ	jiten'sha	bicycle
しんかんせん	shin'kan'sen	Shinkansen / bullet train
ちかてつ	chikatetsu	subway / metro
でんしゃ	den'sha	train
ひこうき	hikooki	airplane
タクシー	takushii	taxi
バス	basu	bus
めいてつ	meetetsu	Meitetsu Railway (private railway company in central Japan)
なんで	nan de	how (with what tools / transportation means)
Expressions:		
いっしょに　どうですか	issho ni doo desu ka	How about (going) together?

Lesson 7 Shootai – Invitation

Japanese	Pronunciation	English
かいます	kaimasu	to buy
かきます	kakimasu	to write
ききます	kikimasu	to listen / to hear
します	shimasu	to do
たべます	tabemasu	to eat
つくります	tsukurimasu	to make
とります	torimasu	to take
のみます	nomimasu	to drink
みます	mimasu	to watch / to see
よみます	yomimasu	to read
えいが	eega	movie
おんがく	on'gaku	music
しゃしん	shashin	photo
てがみ	tegami	letter
テレビ	terebi	TV
スター・ウォーズ	sutaa uoozu	Star Wars
DVD	diibuidii	DVD
ゲーム	geemu	game
ごはん	gohan	meal
あさごはん	asa-gohan	breakfast
ひるごはん	hiru-gohan	lunch
ばんごはん	ban-gohan	dinner
[お] さけ	[o] sake	alcohol / Japanese Sake
ビール	biiru	beer
ワイン	wain	wine
ピザ	piza	pizza
マンゴー	man'goo	mango
まつり	matsuri	festival
くやくしょ	ku-yakusho	ward office
しやくしょ	shi-yakusho	city hall
にゅうかん	nyuukan	immigration bureau

Japanese	Pronunciation	English
びょういん	byooin	hospital
ひとり	hitori	alone
[ご] かぞく	[go] kazoku	[your] family
～と	～to	with
いつも	itsumo	always
こんど	kon'do	next time / this time
とうきょう	tookyoo	Tokyo
Expressions:		
それは　いいですね	sore wa ii desu ne	That's good.
ぜひ	zehi	By all means. / Definitely.
そうですね	soo desu ne	Well... / That's right.
それから	sorekara	after that

Lesson 8 Watashi no Kazoku (1) – My Family (1)

Japanese	Pronunciation	English
あいます	aimasu	to meet
あります	arimasu	(for something) to exist / there is (something) / to have (something)
います	imasu	(for someone) to exist
あげます	agemasu	to give
もらいます	moraimasu	to receive
おくります	okurimasu	to send
かします	kashimasu	to lend
かります	karimasu	to borrow
しらべます	shirabemasu	to examine / to search / to investigate / to check out
でんわします	den'wa shimasu	to make a phone call
メールします	meeru shimasu	to e-mail
りょこうします	ryokoo shimasu	to travel / to go on a trip
あたたかい	atatakai	warm
すずしい	suzushii	cool
さむい	samui	cold
いたい	itai	painful
おおい	ooi	many / much
すくない	sukunai	few / a little / scarce
（せが）たかい	(se ga) takai	tall (person)
やさしい	yasashii	gentle / kind
きびしい	kibishii	strict
ねむい	nemui	sleepy
［お］げんき	[o] gen'ki	healthy / well / peppy
きれい	kiree	beautiful / clean
しずか	shizuka	quiet
にぎやか	nigiyaka	bustling / busy (place) / lively / cheerful
じょうず	joozu	skillful / good at (something)
へた	heta	unskillful / bad at (something)
ゆうめい	yuumee	famous
せ	se	height
ひと	hito	people / person
ぶっか	bukka	(commodity) prices

— 19 —

Japanese	Pronunciation	English
たこやき	takoyaki	octopus dumpling
りょうり	ryoori	cooking / dishes / cuisine
ぼうし	booshi	hat / cap
はな	hana	flower
カード	kaado	card
プレゼント	purezen'to	gift / present
メール	meeru	e-mail
うみ	umi	sea / ocean
ところ	tokoro	place
クリスマス	kurisumasu	Christmas
たんじょうび	tan'joobi	birthday
てんき	ten'ki	weather
てんきよほう	ten'ki yohoo	weather forecast
はれ	hare	clear weather / sunny
あめ	ame	rain
ゆき	yuki	snow
ちち	chichi	my father
はは	haha	my mother
あに	ani	my older brother
あね	ane	my older sister
おとうと	otooto	my younger brother
いもうと	imooto	my younger sister
りょうしん	ryooshin	parents
こいびと	koibito	boyfriend / girlfriend / partner
いしゃ	isha	(medical) doctor
かいしゃいん	kaishain	company employee
きょうし	kyooshi	teacher / instructor
こうこうせい	kookoosee	high school student
だいがくせい	daigakusee	university student

Japanese	Pronunciation	English
ひとり	hitori	one person
ふたり	futari	two people
～にん	～nin	suffix for counting people
いぬ	inu	dog
ねこ	neko	cat
あさくさ	asakusa	Asakusa (a famous tourist district in downtown Tokyo)
おきなわ	okinawa	Okinawa Prefecture
なごや	nagoya	Nagoya City
かんこうち	kan'koochi	tourist spot
ふるさと	furusato	hometown
なつやすみ	natsu-yasumi	summer vacation
ふゆやすみ	fuyu-yasumi	winter vacation
でも	demo	but / however
どんな	don'na	what kind
なに	nani	what
なんにん	nan-nin	how many people
Expressions:		
もうすぐ	moosugu	soon
ひさしぶりですね	hisashiburi desu ne	It's been a long time.

— 21 —

Structural Exercises : oral

1

e.g.) 1. A : Sumimasen, ①toire wa doko desu ka.
   B : ②Asoko desu.
   A : Doomo.

2. A : Sumimasen, ①hon-ya wa doko desu ka.
   B : ②1[i]-kkai desu.
   A : Doomo.

2

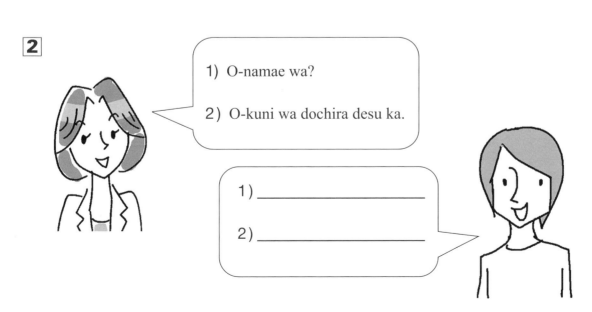

1) O-namae wa?

2) O-kuni wa dochira desu ka.

1) _____

2) _____

3

れい) 1. <u>ろくじ</u>です。
   2. A：なんじですか。
      B：<u>ろくじ</u>です。

4

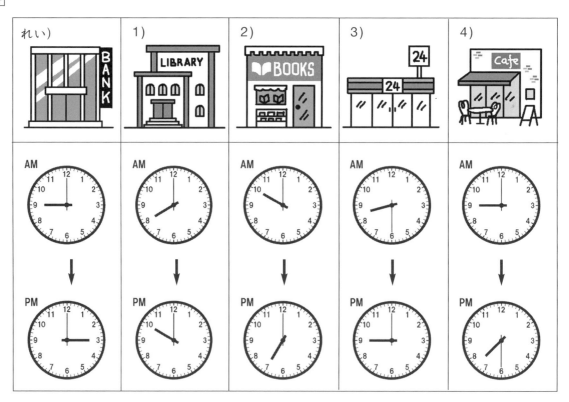

れい) 1. <u>ぎんこう</u>は <u>くじ</u>から <u>ごご さんじ</u>まで です。
   2. A：あの、きょう <u>ぎんこう</u>は なんじまでですか。
      B：<u>ごご さんじ</u>までです。
      A：そうですか。

3

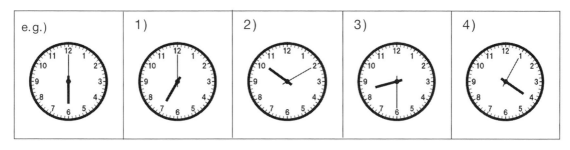

e.g.) 1. <u>6[roku]-ji</u> desu.
    2. A：Nan-ji desu ka.
       B：<u>6[roku]-ji</u> desu.

4

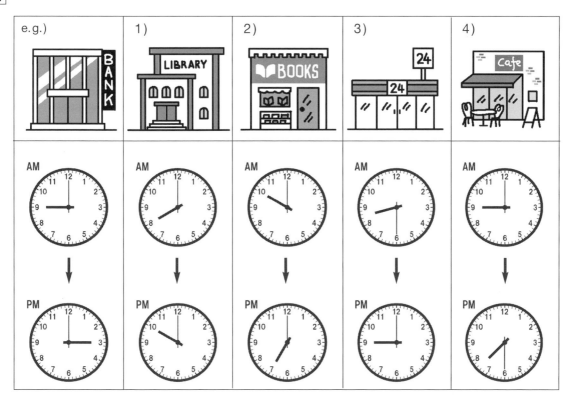

e.g.) 1. <u>Gin'koo</u> wa <u>9[ku]-ji</u> kara <u>gogo 3[san]-ji</u> made desu.
    2. A：Ano, kyoo <u>gin'koo</u> wa nan-ji made desu ka.
       B：<u>Gogo 3[san]-ji</u> made desu.
       A：Soo desu ka.

5

れい) 1. これは　マレーシアの　クッキーです。
　　　2. A：これ、おいしいですね。どこの　クッキーですか。
　　　　　B：マレーシアのです。
　　　　　A：そうですか。

5

e.g.) 1. Kore wa <u>Mareeshia</u> no <u>kukkii</u> desu.
      2. A：Kore, <u>oishii</u> desu ne. Doko no <u>kukkii</u> desu ka.
         B：<u>Mareeshia</u> no desu.
         A：Soo desu ka.

Conversational Exercises :

1. きのう①<u>クラブの　はっぴょう</u>でした。
㉑　<u>クラブ</u>は　②<u>ごご　1じから　3じまで</u>ですが、きのうは　③<u>4じ</u>に
　　おわりました。たいへんでした。

　　1) ①アルバイト　　　　　②ごご　6じ〜10じ　　　③12じ
　　2) ①にほんごの　クラス　②ごぜん　10じ〜12じ　　③ごご1じ
　　3) ①じっけん　　　　　　②ごぜん　10じ〜ごご3じ　③5じ

2. もり　：おはようございます。
㉒　ブディ：おはようございます。
　　もり　：あ、ブディさん、①<u>はやい</u>ですね。②<u>まだ　8じ</u>ですよ。
　　ブディ：はい、③<u>きょうは　6じに　おきました</u>。
　　もり　：<u>6じ</u>！
　　ブディ：はい、きょうは　テストです。
　　もり　：そうですか。がんばって　ください。

　　1) ①おそい　　②もう　12じ　③きのうは　2じに　ねました
　　2) ①はやい　　②まだ　7じ　　③ゼミは　7じはんに　はじまります

Conversational Exercises :

1. Kinoo ①kurabu no happyoo deshita.

Kurabu wa ②gogo 1-ji kara 3-ji made desu ga, kinoo wa ③4-ji ni owarimashita. Taihen deshita.

   1) ① arubaito   ② gogo 6-ji～10-ji   ③ 12-ji
   2) ① Nihon-go no kurasu ② gozen 10-ji～12-ji   ③ gogo 1-ji
   3) ① jikken   ② gozen 10-ji～gogo 3-ji ③ 5-ji

2. Mori : Ohayoo gozaimasu.
Budi : Ohayoo gozaimasu.
Mori : A, Budi-san, ①hayai desu ne. ②Mada 8-ji desu yo.
Budi : Hai, ③kyoo wa 6-ji ni okimashita.
Mori : 6-ji!
Budi : Hai, kyoo wa tesuto desu.
Mori : Soo desu ka. Gan'batte kudasai.

   1) ① osoi   ② moo 12-ji   ③ kinoo wa 2-ji ni nemashita
   2) ① hayai   ② mada 7-ji   ③ zemi wa 7-ji han ni hajimarimasu.

3. ㉓
ハイン　　：あの、すみません。
　　　　　　①としょかんは　なんじから　なんじまでですか。
あんどう　：ごぜん　②10じから　ごご　③9じまでです。
ハイン　　：そうですか。やすみは　なんようびですか。
あんどう　：④にちようびです。
ハイン　　：ありがとうございました。

　　1) ①ATM　　　　②9じ　　　③5じ　　　④どようびと　にちようび
　　2) ①ばいてん　　②10じ　　　③6じ　　　④にちようび

4. ㉔
チン　　　：すみません。あの　メモ、なんて　かいて　ありますか。
たかはし　：はい、えーっと…。「1じから　①はっぴょうの　れんしゅう」
　　　　　　ですよ。
チン　　　：そうですか。②きょうしつは　どこですか。
たかはし　：③215です。
チン　　　：どうも。

　　1) ①こうぎ　　　　　　②きょうしつ　　　③361
　　2) ①うちあわせ／かいぎ　②かいぎしつ　　　③218

— 70 —

3.   Hain   : Ano, sumimasen.
            ①Toshokan wa nan-ji kara nan-ji made desu ka.
   Andoo : Gozen ②10-ji kara gogo ③9-ji made desu.
   Hain   : Soo desu ka. Yasumi wa nan-yoobi desu ka.
   Andoo : ④Nichi-yoobi desu.
   Hain   : Arigatoo gozaimashita.

   1) ① ATM   ② 9-ji   ③ 5-ji   ④ do-yoobi to nichi-yoobi
   2) ① baiten   ② 10-ji   ③ 6-ji   ④ nichi-yoobi

4.   Chin   : Sumimasen. Ano memo, nan'te kaite arimasu ka.
   Takahashi : Hai, eetto…. "1-ji kara ① happyoo no ren'shuu" desu yo.
   Chin   : Soo desu ka. ②Kyooshitsu wa doko desu ka.
   Takahashi : ③215 desu.
   Chin   : Doomo.

   1) ① koogi   ② kyooshitsu   ③ 361
   2) ① uchiawase / kaigi ② kaigishitsu   ③ 218

5. アン ：あの、みなさん、これ、どうぞ。
㉕　もり ：え！？　なんですか。
　　アン ：①とうきょうの　おみやげです。②キャンディーですよ。
　　もり ：わあ、ありがとうございます。

　　１）①おおさか　　　　　②クッキー
　　２）①ほっかいどう　　　②チョコレート

5. An   : Ano, mina-san, kore, doozo.
⑤   Mori : Eh!? Nan desu ka.
　　An   : ①Tookyoo no omiyage desu. ②Kyan'dii desu yo.
　　Mori : Waa, arigatoo gozaimasu.

　　1) ① Oosaka　　② kukkii
　　2) ① Hokkaidoo　② chokoreeto

Structural Exercices : writing

1. 1)【 8じ ・ は ・ から ・ です ・ ぎんこう ・ ごぜん 】

→_____

2)【 きて ・ に ・ 1じはん ・ ください 】

→_____

3)【 やすみ ・ にちようび ・ は ・ ばいてん ・ です ・ の 】

→_____

4)【 これ ・ の ・ おみやげ ・ は ・ マレーシア ・ です 】

→_____

5)【 べんきょうします ・ くじ ・ から ・ まで ・ じゅういちじ 】

→_____

2. れい)【 がくせい ・ もり ・ せんせい 】

A：すみません。あの　ひとは　どなたですか。

B：＿もりさん＿です。

1)【 はじまります ・ おわります ・ べんきょうします 】

にほんごの　クラスは　9じに ＿＿＿＿＿＿＿＿＿。

そして、12じに ＿＿＿＿＿＿＿＿＿。

2)【 に ・ から ・ ごぜん ・ まで ・ ごご 】

としょかんは ＿＿＿＿＿ 9じから ＿＿＿＿＿ 10じまでです。

わたしは　ごご　8じ＿＿＿＿＿ 10じ ＿＿＿＿＿ べんきょうします。

— 74 —

Structural Exercices : writing

1. 1) 【 8-ji ・ wa ・ kara ・ desu ・ gin'koo ・ gozen 】

→_____

2) 【 kite ・ ni ・ 1-ji han ・ kudasai 】

→_____

3) 【 yasumi ・ nichi-yoobi ・ wa ・ baiten ・ desu ・ no 】

→_____

4) 【 kore ・ no ・ omiyage ・ wa ・ Mareeshia ・ desu 】

→_____

5) 【 ben'kyooshimasu ・ 9-ji ・ kara ・ made ・ 11-ji 】

→_____

2. e.g.) 【 gakusee ・ Mori ・ sen'see 】

A : Sumimasen. Ano hito wa donata desu ka.

B : _Mori-san_ desu.

1) 【 hajimarimasu ・ owarimasu ・ ben'kyooshimasu 】

Nihon-go no kurasu wa 9-ji ni _____ .

Soshite, 12-ji ni _____ .

2) 【 ni ・ kara ・ gozen ・ made ・ gogo 】

Toshokan wa _____ 9-ji kara _____ 10-ji made desu.

Watashi wa gogo 8-ji _____ 10-ji _____ ben'kyooshimasu.

3. れい） A：これは＿＿なん＿＿ですか。

　　　　 B：ほんです。

1) A：じっけんは ＿＿＿＿＿＿＿＿＿＿ から　です か。

　 B：8じからです。

2) A：ATMは ＿＿＿＿＿＿＿＿＿ まで　です か。

　 B：ごご5じまでです。

3) A：やすみは ＿＿＿＿＿＿＿＿＿ です か。

　 B：にちようびです。

4) A：203の　きょうしつは ＿＿＿＿＿＿＿＿＿ です か。

　 B：あそこです。

4. 1)

┌───┐
│ じむしつ   │
│ 8：30〜17：00　　※　どようび・にちようびは　やすみ │
└───┘

A：すみません、＿＿＿＿＿＿＿＿＿＿ は　なんじからですか。

B：＿＿＿＿＿＿＿＿＿ からですよ。

A：なんじまでですか。

B：＿＿＿＿＿＿＿＿＿ までですよ。

A：やすみは　なんようびですか？

B：＿＿＿＿＿＿＿＿＿ と ＿＿＿＿＿＿＿＿＿ です。

2) A：すみません、あのメモ、なんて　かいてありますか。

　 B：えーっと・・・、「ごご　2じはんから　テスト」ですよ。

　 A：テストの　きょうしつは ＿＿＿＿＿＿＿＿＿＿＿ 。

　 B：302きょうしつです。

┌──────────┐
│ 日本語   │
│ テスト   │
│ 14：30 〜   │
│ @302   │
└──────────┘

3. e.g.)   A：Kore wa <u>nan</u> desu ka.
　　　　　B：Hon desu.

1) A：Jikken wa _____ kara desu ka.
　 B：8-ji kara desu.

2) A：ATM wa _____ made desu ka.
　 B：Gogo 5-ji made desu.

3) A：Yasumi wa _____ desu ka.
　 B：Nichi-yoobi desu.

4) A：203 no kyooshitsu wa _____ desu ka.
　 B：Asoko desu.

4.

1)
┌───┐
│ jimu-shitsu   │
│ 8：30〜17：00 ※ do-yoobi・nichi-yoobi wa yasumi │
└───┘

　 A：Sumimasen, _____ wa nan-ji kara desu ka.
　 B：_____ kara desu yo.
　 A：Nan-ji made desu ka.
　 B：_____ made desu yo.
　 A：Yasumi wa nan-yoobi desu ka.
　 B：_____ to _____ desu.

2)
　 A：Sumimasen, ano memo, nan'te kaitearimasu ka.
　 B：Eetto…, "gogo 2-ji han kara tesuto" desu yo.
　 A：Tesuto no kyooshitsu wa _____ .
　 B：302 kyooshitsu desu.

┌─────────────┐
│ 日本語   │
│ テスト   │
│ 14 :30 〜   │
│ @302   │
└─────────────┘

3) A：あのう、これ・・・。
　　B：え！？　なんですか。
　　A：_____ です。_____ のおみやげです。
　　　みなさん、どうぞ。
　　B：わあ、ありがとうございます。

4) A：あのう、これ、どうぞ。
　　B：わあ、これ、なんですか。
　　A：_____ の_____ です。
　　B：ありがとうございます。いただきます。

3) A : Anoo, kore….
   B : E!? Nan desu ka.
   A : _____ desu. _____ no omiyage desu. Mina-san, doozo.
   B : Waa, arigatoo gozaimasu.

4) A : Anoo, kore, doozo.
   B : Waa, kore, nan desu ka.
   A : _____ no _____ desu.
   B : Arigatoo gozaimasu. Itadakimasu.

3) Kyooto ・ okashi
4) (?) ・ (?)

Lesson 6

はっぴょう
Presentation

> **Targets:**
> ✓ Can explain your own plan or schedule.
> ✓ Can explain someone else's plan or schedule.
> ✓ Can talk about your past experiences.

Model Conversation : ㉖

<じっけんしつで>

アン　　：　うーん・・・・。
ハイン：　あ、アンさん。いそがしそうですね。
アン　　：　はい、らいげつ　ちゅうがっこうに　いきます。
　　　　　　そして、スピーチします。
　　　　　　ハインさんは　いきますか。
ハイン：　はい、いきますよ。
アン　　：　そうですか。なんで　いきますか。
ハイン：　くるまで　いきます。あ、アンさんも　いっしょに　どうですか。
アン　　：　えっ！？　いいですか。おねがいします。

-・-・-・-・-・-・-・-・-・-・-・-・-・-・-・-・-・-・-

<よる、レストランで>

ブディ：　アンさん、じゅんびしましたか。
アン　　：　はい、きのう　てつやしました。
ブディ：　そうですか。たいへんですね。

Lesson 6

Happyoo
Presentation

Targets :
- ✓ Can explain your own plan or schedule.
- ✓ Can explain someone else's plan or schedule.
- ✓ Can talk about your past experiences.

Model Conversation : ㉖

< Jikken'shitsu de >

An　　：　Uun….

Hain　：　A, An-san. Isogashisoo desu ne.

An　　：　Hai, rai-getsu chuugakkoo ni ikimasu.
　　　　　Soshite, supiichishimasu.
　　　　　Hain-san wa ikimasu ka.

Hain　：　Hai, ikimasu yo.

An　　：　Soo desu ka. Nan de ikimasu ka.

Hain　：　Kuruma de ikimasu. A, An-san mo issho ni doo desu ka.

An　　：　Eh!? Ii desu ka. Onegaishimasu.

―――――――――――――――――――――――

< Yoru, resutoran de >

Budi　：　An-san, jun'bishimashita ka.

An　　：　Hai, kinoo tetsuyashimashita.

Budi　：　Soo desu ka. Taihen desu ne.

Structural Exercises : oral

1

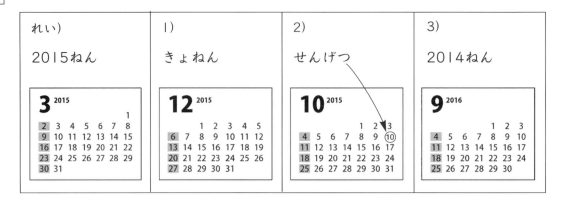

れい) 1. 2015ねんの 3がつ
　　 2. A：いつ にほんに きましたか。
　　　　B：2015ねんの 3がつに きました。

2

れい) 1. さかえに いきます。
　　 2. ちかてつで さかえに いきます

Structural Exercises : oral

1

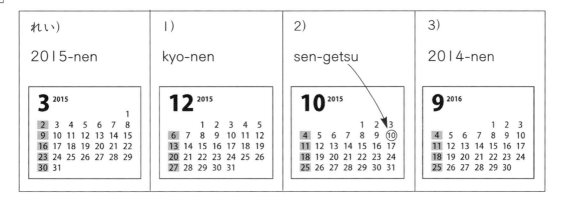

e.g.) 1. <u>2015-nen</u> no <u>3-gatsu</u>

2. A : Itsu Nihon ni kimashita ka.

   B : <u>2015nen no 3-gatsu</u> ni kimashita.

2

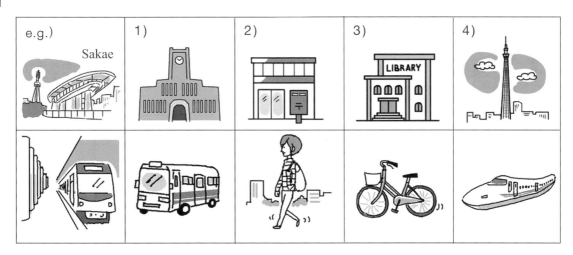

e.g.) 1. <u>Sakae</u> ni ikimasu.

2. <u>Chikatetsu</u> de <u>Sakae</u> ni ikimasu.

3

れい）　Ａ：きのう　どこに　いきましたか。

　　　　Ｂ：①スーパーに　いきました。

　　　　Ａ：なんで　いきましたか。

　　　　Ｂ：②じてんしゃで　いきました。

　　1)　①さかえ　　　　　②ちかてつ

　　2)　①おおす　　　　　②ともだちの　くるま

　　3)　①きょうと　　　　②バス

4

れい）　Ａ：いそがしそうですね。①しゅくだいですか。

　　　　Ｂ：はい、あした②PPTで　はっぴょうします。

　　　　Ａ：そうですか。

　　1)　①レポート　　　　②えいご

　　2)　①しゅくだい　　　②にほんご

3

e.g.)　A : Kinoo doko ni ikimashita ka.

　　　B : ①Suupaa ni ikimashita

　　　A : Nan de ikimashita ka.

　　　B : ②Jitensha de ikimashita.

1)　① Sakae　　　　② chikatetsu

2)　① Oosu　　　　② tomodachi no kuruma

3)　① Kyooto　　　② basu

4

e.g.)　A : Isogashisoo desu ne.　①Shukudai desu ka.

　　　B : Hai, ashita②PPT de happyooshimasu.

　　　A : Soo desu ka.

1)　① repooto　　　② Ee-go

2)　① shukudai　　② Nihon-go

Conversational Exercises :

1. ブディ：アンさん、いそがしそうですね。①しゅくだいですか。
㉗ アン　：はい、あした　②PPTで　はっぴょうします。
　　ブディ：そうですか。がんばって　ください。

　　　1) ①レポート　　　②にほんご
　　　2) ①しゅくだい　　②えいご

2. まいあさ　①9じに　クラブに　いきます。
㉘ ②9じはんから　12じまで　テニスします。
　　かいわの　クラスは　すいようびの　ごご　1じ　からです。
　　③PPTで　はっぴょうします。
　　6じに　おわります。そして、みんなで
　　いっしょに　④いざかやに　いきます。

　　　1) ①10じ　としょかん
　　　　 ②10じ〜12じ　べんきょうします
　　　　 ③にほんご
　　　　 ④カラオケ
　　　2) ①8じ　2ごうかん
　　　　 ②9じ〜16じ　けんきゅうします
　　　　 ③えいご
　　　　 ④レストラン

3. チン：あした　①おおすに　いきますか。
㉙ もり：はい、いきますよ。
　　チン：そうですか。なんで　いきますか。
　　もり：②ちかてつで　いきます。チンさんも　いっしょに　どうですか。
　　チン：ありがとうございます。なんじに　いきますか。
　　もり：③10じに　いきましょう。

　　　1) ①さかえ　　　　②バス　　　　　　　　③1じはん
　　　2) ①きょうと　　　②せんぱいの　くるま　③9じ

— 86 —

Conversational Exercises :

1. Budi : An-san, isogashisoo desu ne. ①Shukudai desu ka.
㉗
　　An　 : Hai, ashita ②PPT de happyooshimasu.

　　Budi : Soo desu ka. Gan'batte kudasai.

　　1) ① repooto　　② Nihon-go
　　2) ① shukudai　　② Ee-go

2. Mai-asa ①9-ji ni kurabu ni ikimasu.
㉘
②9-ji han kara 12-ji made tenisushimasu.

Kaiwa no kurasu wa sui-yoobi no gogo 1-ji kara desu.

③PPT de happyooshimasu.

6-ji ni owarimasu. Soshite, min'na de

issho ni ④izakaya ni ikimasu.

　　1) ① 10-ji　toshokan
　　　 ② 10-ji〜1-ji ben'kyooshimasu
　　　 ③ Nihon-go
　　　 ④ karaoke
　　2) ① 8-ji　2-gookan
　　　 ② 9-ji〜16-ji ken'kyuushimasu
　　　 ③ Ee-go
　　　 ④ resutoran

3. Chin : Ashita ①Oosu ni ikimasu ka.
㉙
　　Mori : Hai, ikimasu yo.

　　Chin : Soo desu ka. Nan de ikimasu ka.

　　Mori : ②Chikatetsu de ikimasu. Chin-san mo issho ni doo desu ka.

　　Chin : Arigatoo gozaimasu. Nan-ji ni ikimasu ka.

　　Mori : ③10-ji ni ikimashoo.

　　1) ① Sakae　　② basu　　　　　　　③ 1-ji han
　　2) ① Kyooto　 ② sen'pai no kuruma　③ 9-ji

Structural Exercices : writing

1. れい)【やすみます・は・ブディさん・あした】
　　　→<u>ブディさんは　あした　やすみます。</u>

　1)【だいがく・に・まいにち・くじ・いきます・に】
　　→_____

　2)【ゆうびんきょく・バス・に・いきます・で】
　　→_____

2.

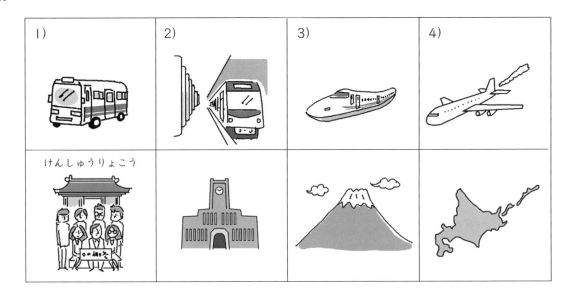

　1) あした _____ で _____ に いきます。
　2) まいにち _____ で _____ に いきます。
　3) きのう _____ で _____ に いきました。
　4) せんしゅう _____ で _____ に いきました。

Structural Exercices : writing

1. e.g.) 【 yasumimasu・wa・Budi-san・ashita 】

→ Budi-san wa ashita yasumimasu.

1) 【 daigaku・ni・mai-nichi・9-ji・ikimasu・ni 】

→ _____

2) 【 yuubin'kyoku・basu・ni・ikimasu・de 】

→ _____

2.

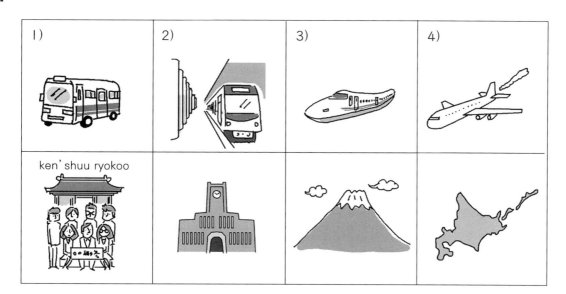

1) Ashita _____ de _____ ni ikimasu.

2) Mai-nichi _____ de _____ ni ikimasu.

3) Kinoo _____ de _____ ni ikimashita.

4) Sen-shuu _____ de _____ ni ikimashita

3. 1) A：＿＿＿＿＿＿＿＿＿＿＿　はっぴょうしますか。

　　　B：PPTで　はっぴょうします。

　　2) A：＿＿＿＿＿＿＿＿＿＿＿くにへ　かえりますか。

　　　B：ひこうきで　かえります。

　　3) A：＿＿＿＿＿＿＿＿＿＿＿　にほんに　きましたか。

　　　B：きょねんの　10がつに　きました。

4. 1)【じゅうじ　・　にほんご　・　クラス】

　　　A：あした＿＿＿＿＿＿＿＿＿＿＿　で　はっぴょうします。

　　　B：えいごで　はっぴょうしますか。

　　　A：いいえ、＿＿＿＿＿＿＿＿＿＿＿で　はっぴょうします。

　　　＿＿＿＿＿＿＿＿＿＿＿からです。

　　　B：がんばってください。

　　2)【いっしょ　・　くるま　・　けんきゅうかい】

　　　A：あした＿＿＿＿＿＿＿＿＿＿＿　に　いきますか。

　　　B：はい、いきますよ。

　　　A：わたしは＿＿＿＿＿＿＿＿＿＿＿　で　いきます。

　　　Bさんも、　　　＿＿＿＿＿＿＿＿＿＿＿　に　どうぞ。

　　　B：わあ、ありがとうございます。

3. 1) A : _____ happyooshimasu ka.

B : PPT de happyooshimasu.

2) A : _____ kuni e kaerimasu ka.

B : Hikooki de kaerimasu.

3) A : _____ Nihon ni kimashita ka.

B : Kyo-nen no 10-gatsu ni kimashita.

4. 1) 【 10-ji ・ Nihon-go ・ kurasu 】

A : Ashita _____ de happyooshimasu.

B : Ee-go de happyooshimasu ka.

A : Iie, _____ de happyooshimasu.

_____ kara desu.

B : Gan'batte kudasai.

2) 【 issho ・ kuruma ・ ken'kyuu-kai 】

A : Ashita _____ ni ikimasu ka.

B : Hai, ikimasu yo.

A : Watashi wa _____ de ikimasu.

B-san mo, _____ ni doozo.

B : Waa, arigatoo gozaimasu.

— 91 —

5. <u>ひらがなで</u> かきましょう。

1)

2 20XX

1	2	3	4	5	6	7
8	9	10	11	12	13	14
15	16	17	18	19	20	21
22	23	24	25	26	27	28

2)

3 20XX

1	2	3	4	5	6	7
8	9	10	11	12	13	14
15	16	17	18	19	20	21
22	23	24	25	26	27	28

3)-①

12 20XX

	1	2	3	4	5	6
7	8	9	10	11	12	13
14	15	16	17	18	19	20
21	22	23	24	25	26	27
28	29	30	31

②

1 20XX

	1	2	3	4
5	6	7	8	9	10	11
12	13	14	15	16	17	18
19	20	21	22	23	24	25
26	27	28	29	30	31

1) A：いつ　けんきゅうかいで　はっぴょうしましたか。
　　B：きょねんの _____ 。

2) A：いつ　くにに　かえりますか。
　　B：らいねんの _____ 。

3) A：ふゆやすみは　いつですか。
　　B：① _____ から　② _____ までです。

6.　しつもんに　こたえましょう。

1) きのう　なんじに　ねましたか。

2) きょう　なんじに　おきましたか。

3) きょう　なんで　だいがくに　きましたか。

4) あした　どこに　いきますか。

5) いつ　くにに　かえりますか。

6) たんじょうびは　いつですか。

5. Rooma-ji de kakimashoo.

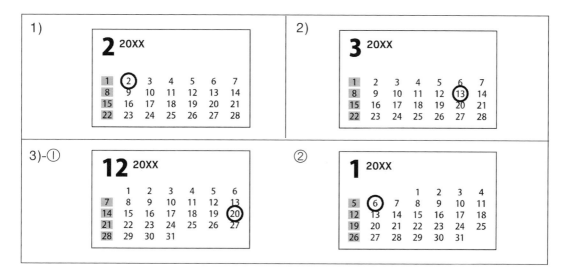

1) A : Itsu ken'kyuu-kai de happyooshimashita ka.
   B : Kyo-nen no _____ .

2) A : Itsu kuni ni kaerimasu ka.
   B : Rai-nen no _____ .

3) A : Fuyu-yasumi wa itsu desu ka.
   B : ① _____ kara ② _____ made desu.

6. Shitsumon ni kotaemashoo.

1) Kinoo nan-ji ni nemashita ka.

2) Kyoo nan-ji ni okimashita ka.

3) Kyoo nan de daigaku ni kimashita ka.

4) Ashita doko ni ikimasu ka.

5) Itsu kuni ni kaerimasu ka.

6) Tan'joobi wa itsu desu ka.

Lesson 7

しょうたい
Invitation

> **Targets:**
> ✓ Can make and respond to invitations and suggestions.
> ✓ Can discuss what to do, where to go and make arrangements to meet.

Model Conversation: ㉚

＜きょうしつで＞

たかはし： ブディさん　なんの　おんがくですか。

ブディ　： あ、マレーシアの　おんがくです。

たかはし： へえ、いいですね。

ブディ　： たかはしさん、こんど　うちに　きませんか。
　　　　　　うちで　いっしょに　CDを　ききましょう。

たかはし： わあ、それは　いいですね。ぜひ、おねがいします。

─・─・─・─・─・─・─・─・─・─・─・─・─・─・─・─・─・─

＜ブディさんの　うちで＞

たかはし： いい　おんがくですね。

ブディ　： ありがとう。
　　　　　　たかはしさん、この　ジュース　のみませんか。

たかはし： これは　なんですか。

ブディ　： これは　マレーシアの　マンゴージュースです。
　　　　　　おいしいですよ。

たかはし： じゃ、いただきます。

— 94 —

Lesson 7

Shootai
Invitation

> **Targets :**
> ✓ Can make and respond to invitations and suggestions.
> ✓ Can discuss what to do, where to go and make arrangements to meet.

Model Conversation : ㉚

＜Kyooshitsu de＞

Takahashi	:	Budi-san nan no on'gaku desu ka.
Budi	:	A, Mareeshia no on'gaku desu.
Takahashi	:	Hee, ii desu ne.
Budi	:	Takahashi-san, kon'do uchi ni kimasen ka.
		Uchi de issho ni CD o kikimashoo.
Takahashi	:	Waa, sore wa ii desu ne. Zehi, onegaishimasu.

＜Budi-san no uchi de＞

Takahashi	:	Ii on'gaku desu ne.
Budi	:	Arigatoo.
		Takahashi-san, kono juusu o nomimasen ka.
Takahashi	:	Kore wa nan desu ka.
Budi	:	Kore wa Mareeshia no man'goo juusu desu.
		Oishii desu yo.
Takahashi	:	Ja, itadakimasu.

Structural Exercises : oral

1 なにを しますか。

れい） 1. ともだちと ごはんを たべます。
2. A：やすみのひに なにを しますか。
   B：ともだちと ごはんを たべます。
3. A：きのう なにを しましたか。
   B：ともだちと ごはんを たべました。
4. しょくどうで ごはんを たべます。
5. ともだちと しょくどうで ごはんを たべます。
6. A：どこで ごはんを たべますか。
   B：しょくどうで たべます。
   A：だれと たべますか。
   B：ともだちと たべます。

2

れい）　A：にちようびに ①きょうとに いきました。
　　　B：いいですね。だれと いきましたか。
　　　A：②ともだちと いきました。
　　　B：そうですか。どうでしたか。
　　　A：③たのしかったです。

1) ①とうきょう　　②ゼミの せんぱい　　③おもしろい
2) ①おまつり（に）　②にほんじんの ともだち　③いい

3

れい）　A：Bさん、①あしたは パーティーですよ。
　　　　いっしょに ②いきませんか。
　　　B：いいですね。②いきましょう。

1) ①にちようびは バーベキュー　　②いきます
2) ①この DVDは おもしろい　　　②みます
3) ①この ケーキは おいしい　　　②たべます
4) ①この ワインは おいしい　　　②のみます

Structural Exercises : oral

1 Nani o shimasu ka.

e.g.) 1. Tomodachi to gohan o tabemasu.
2. A : Yasumi no hi ni nani o shimasu ka.
   B : Tomodachi to gohan o tabemasu.
3. A : Kinoo nani o shimashita ka.
   B : Tomodachi to gohan o tabemashita.
4. Shokudoo de gohan o tabemasu.
5. Tomodachi to Shokudoo de gohan o tabemasu.
6. A : Doko de gohan o tabemasuka.
   B : Shokudoo de tabemasu.
   A : Dare to tabemasuka.
   B : Tomodachi to tabemasu.

2

e.g.) A : Nichi-yoobi ni ①Kyooto ni ikimashita.
B : Ii desu ne. Dare to ikimashitaka.
A : ②Tomodachi to ikimasu.
B : Soo desu ka.
A : ③Tanoshikatta desu.

1) ① Tookyoo   ② zemi no sen'pai   ③ omoshiroi
2) ① o-matsuri(ni)   ② Nihon-jin no tomodachi ③ ii

3

e.g.) A : B-san, ①ashita wa paatii desuyo.
        Issho ni ②ikimasen ka.
      B : Ii desu ne. ②Ikimashoo.

1) ① nichi-yoobi wa baabekyuu   ② ikimasu
2) ① Kono DVD wa omoshiroi   ② mimasu
3) ① Kono keeki wa oishii   ② tabemasu
4) ① Kono wain wa oishii   ② nomimasu

Conversational Exercises:

1. せんせい：おはようございます。
㉛　ハイン　：あの、きょう①<u>チンさん</u>は　やすみます。
　　せんせい：そうですか。
　　ハイン　：はい、②<u>しやくしょ</u>に　いきます。
　　せんせい：ああ、わかりました。ひとりで　いきますか。
　　ハイン　：いいえ、③<u>ミンさん</u>と　いっしょに　いきます。
　　せんせい：そうですか。

　　1) ①ブディさん　　②けんきゅうかい　　③たかはしさん
　　2) ①アンさん　　　②びょういん　　　　③じょしゅの　あんどうさん

2. ミン　：①<u>カラオケに　いき</u>ませんか。
㉜　さとう：いいですね。②<u>いつ</u>　いきましょうか。
　　ミン　：そうですね。③<u>どようび</u>は　どうですか。
　　さとう：いいですね。そうしましょう。

　　1) ①えいがを　みます　　②なにを　みます　　③スターウォーズ
　　2) ①ごはんを　たべます　②なにを　たべます　③ピザ

3. ブディ：こんどの　どようびに　りょうで　パーティーを　しませんか。
㉝　アン　：そうですね。なにを　しますか。
　　ブディ：①<u>ピザを　たべ</u>ましょう。
　　もり　：②<u>ビールも　のみ</u>ましょう。
　　　　　　それから　みんなで　③<u>おんがくを　きき</u>ましょう。
　　アン　：いいですね。

　　1) ①サンドイッチを　つくります
　　　　②ワインも　のみます
　　　　③しゃしんを　とります
　　2) ①からあげを　かいます
　　　　②おにぎりも　つくります
　　　　③ゲームを　します

— 98 —

Conversational Exercises:

1.
sen'see : Ohayoo gozaimasu.
Hain : Ano, kyoo ①Chin-san wa yasumimasu.
sen'see : Soo desu ka.
Hain : Hai, ②shiyakusho ni ikimasu.
sen'see : Aa, wakarimashita. Hitori de ikimasu ka.
Hain : Iie, ③Min-san to issho ni ikimasu.
sen'see : Soo desu ka.

    1) ① Budi-san   ② ken'kyuu-kai   ③ Takahashi-san
    2) ① An-san   ② byooin   ③ joshu no An'doo-san

2.
Min : ①Karaoke ni ikimasen ka.
Satoo : Ii desu ne. ②Itsu ikimashoo ka.
Min : Soo desu ne. ③Do-yoobi wa doo desu ka.
Satoo : Ii desu ne. Soo shimashoo.

    1) ① eega o mimasu   ② nani o mimasu   ③ sutaawoozu
    2) ① gohan o tabemasu   ② nani o tabemasu   ③ piza

3.
Budi : Kon'do no do-yoobi ni ryoo de paatii o shimasen ka.
An : Soo desu ne. Nani o shimasu ka.
Budi : ①Piza o tabemashoo.
Mori : ②Biiru mo nomimashoo.
      Sore kara min'na de ③on'gaku o kikimashoo.
An : Ii desu ne.

    1) ① san'doicchi o tsukurimasu
        ② wain mo nomimasu
        ③ shashin o torimasu
    2) ① kara'age o kaimasu
        ② onigiri mo tsukurimasu
        ③ geemu o shimasu

7　しょうたい / Shootai / Invitation

Structural Exercices : writing

1. れい)【 あした ・ くじ ・ は ・ じゅぎょう ・ から ・ です ・ の 】
　　　→ あしたの　じゅぎょうは　くじからです。

　1)【 コンサート ・ に ・ いきませんか ・ こんど 】
　　→＿＿＿＿＿＿＿＿＿＿＿＿＿＿＿＿＿＿＿＿＿＿＿＿＿＿＿＿＿

　2)【 に ・ しゃしん ・ を ・ いっしょ ・ とりましょう 】
　　→＿＿＿＿＿＿＿＿＿＿＿＿＿＿＿＿＿＿＿＿＿＿＿＿＿＿＿＿＿

　3)【 で ・ うち ・ たべました ・ ピザ ・ を 】
　　→＿＿＿＿＿＿＿＿＿＿＿＿＿＿＿＿＿＿＿＿＿＿＿＿＿＿＿＿＿

　4)【 と ・ チンさん ・ に ・ がっかい ・ いきました 】
　　→＿＿＿＿＿＿＿＿＿＿＿＿＿＿＿＿＿＿＿＿＿＿＿＿＿＿＿＿＿

2. 1)　　【 なんで ・ いきます ・ じてんしゃ 】
　　　　A：いまから、ゼミの みんなと さかえの カラオケに いきます。
　　　　　 たかはしさんは いきますか。
　　　　B：はい、＿＿＿＿＿＿＿＿＿＿＿＿＿＿＿＿＿。
　　　　A：そうですか。＿＿＿＿＿＿＿＿＿＿＿＿＿＿＿ いきますか。
　　　　B：＿＿＿＿＿＿＿＿＿＿＿＿＿＿ で いきます。

　2)　　【 うち ・ ビール ・ えいが ・ ともだち 】
　　　　A：きのう＿＿＿＿＿＿＿＿＿ が ＿＿＿＿＿＿＿＿＿ に きました。
　　　　B：へえ、なにを しましたか。
　　　　A：いっしょに ＿＿＿＿＿＿＿＿＿ を みました。
　　　　　 そして、＿＿＿＿＿＿＿＿ を のみました。とても たのしかったです。
　　　　B：よかったですね。

　3)　　【 いきましょう ・ いきませんか ・ たべますか ・ たべませんか 】
　　　　A：きょう ひるごはんを いっしょに ＿＿＿＿＿＿＿＿＿＿＿＿＿＿。
　　　　B：いいですよ。どこで ＿＿＿＿＿＿＿＿＿＿＿＿＿。
　　　　A：さくらずしに ＿＿＿＿＿＿＿＿＿＿＿＿。
　　　　B：いいですね。＿＿＿＿＿＿＿＿＿＿＿＿。

　4)　　【 いきます ・ やすみます ・ わかりました 】
　　　　A：せんせい、きょう さとうさんは ＿＿＿＿＿＿＿＿＿＿＿＿＿＿。
　　　　B：そうですか。
　　　　A：はい、しやくしょに ＿＿＿＿＿＿＿＿＿＿＿＿＿。
　　　　B：＿＿＿＿＿＿＿＿＿＿＿＿。

Structural Exercices : writing

1. e.g.)【ashita ・ 9-ji ・ wa ・ jugyoo ・ kara・ desu ・ no 】

　　　→Ashita no jugyoo wa 9-ji kara desu.

1)【kon'saato ・ ni ・ ikimasen ka ・ kon'do 】

　　→_____

2)【ni ・ shashin ・ o ・ issho ・ torimashoo 】

　　→_____

3)【de ・ uchi ・ tabemashita ・ piza ・ o 】

　　→_____

4)【to ・ Chin-san ・ ni ・ ga-kkai ・ ikimashita 】

　　→_____

2. 1)　【nan-de ・ ikimasu ・ jiten'sha 】

　　A : Ima kara, zemi no min'na to Sakae no karaok ni ikimasu.

　　　　Takahashi-san wa ikimasu ka.

　　B : Hai, _____ .

　　A : Soo desu ka. _____ ikimasu ka.

　　B : _____ de ikimasu.

2)　【uchi ・ biiru ・ eega ・ tomodachi 】

　　A : Kinoo _____ ga _____ ni kimashita.

　　B : Hee, nani o shimashita ka.

　　A : Issho ni _____ o mimashita.

　　　Soshite, _____ o nomimashita. Totemo tanoshikatta desu.

　　B : Yokatta desu ne.

3)　【ikimashoo ・ ikimasen ka ・ tabemasu ka ・ tabemasen ka 】

　　A : Kyoo hiru-gohan o issho ni _____ .

　　B : Ii desu yo. Doko de _____ .

　　A : Sakura-zushi ni _____ .

　　B : Ii desu ne. _____ .

4)　【ikimasu ・ yasumimasu ・ wakarimashita 】

　　A : Sen'see, kyoo Satoo-san wa _____ .

　　B : Soo desu ka.

　　A : Hai, shi-yakusho ni _____ .

　　B : _____ .

7

しょうたい / Shootai / Invitation

3. 1) きのう　ハンバーガー【 を ・ に 】　たべました。

2) コンビニ【 に ・ で 】　おちゃ【 を ・ に 】　かいました。

3) さかえ【 に ・ で 】　ともだち【 を ・ に 】　あいました。

4) きのう　カラオケ【 を ・ に 】　いきました。

4. しつもんに　こたえましょう。

1) きのうの　よる　なにを　たべましたか。

2) らいしゅうの　にちようびに　なにを　しますか。

3) きのう　だれに　あいましたか。

4) まいにち　どこで　しゅくだいを　しますか。

3. 1) Kinoo han'baagaa 【o ・ ni】 tabemashita.

2) Kon'bini 【ni ・ de】 o-cha 【o ・ ni】 kaimashita.

3) Sakae 【ni ・ de】 tomodachi 【o ・ ni】 aimashita.

4) Kinoo karaoke 【o ・ ni】 ikimashita.

4. Shitsumon ni kotaemashoo.

1) Kinoo no yoru nani o tabemashita ka.

2) Raishuu no nichi-yoobini nani o shimasu ka.

3) Kinoo dare ni aimashita ka.

4) Mai-nichi doko de shukudai o shimasu ka.

Lesson 8

わたしの かぞく (1)
My Family (1)

> **Targets :**
> ✓ Can ask how people are and react.
> ✓ Can briefly talk about your family (the number of people, member's occupations, etc.).
> ✓ Can make comments on giving and receiving things (such as presents) and understand such comments.
> ✓ Can greet a friend or a neighbour by mentioning the day's weather with basic expressions.

Model Conversation : ㉞

さとう： アンさん、ひさしぶりですね。
アン ： ええ、きのう くにから かえりました。
　　　　にほんは さむいですね。
さとう： そうですね。でも、てんきは いいですよ。
　　　　ごかぞくは おげんきでしたか。
アン ： ありがとうございます。
　　　　みんな げんきでした。
さとう： おねえさんは？
アン ： あねも とても げんきです。
　　　　この かばんを もらいました。
さとう： わあ、きれいですね。いいですね。
アン ： はい、たんじょうびの プレゼントです。
さとう： やさしい おねえさんですね。

Lesson 8

Watashi no Kazoku (1)
My Family (1)

Targets :
- ✓ Can ask how people are and react.
- ✓ Can briefly talk about your family (the number of people, member's occupations, etc.).
- ✓ Can make comments on giving and receiving things (such as presents) and understand such comments.
- ✓ Can greet a friend or a neighbour by mentioning the day's weather with basic expressions.

Model Conversation : ㉞

Satoo : An-san, hisashiburi desu ne.

An : Ee, kinoo kuni kara kaerimashita.
Nihon wa samui desu ne.

Satoo : Soo desu ne. Demo, ten'ki wa ii desu yo.
Go-kazoku wa o-gen'ki deshita ka.

An : Arigatoo gozaimasu.
Min'na gen'ki deshita.

Satoo : Onee-san wa?

An : Ane mo totemo gen'ki desu.
Kono kaban o moraimashita.

Satoo : Waa, kiree desu ne. Ii desu ne.

An : Hai, tan'joobi no purezen'to desu.

Satoo : Yasashii onee-san desu ne.

Structural Exercises : oral

1

れい) 1. この りょうりは とても <u>すくない</u>です。
　　 2. この りょうりは とても <u>すくなかった</u>です。

2

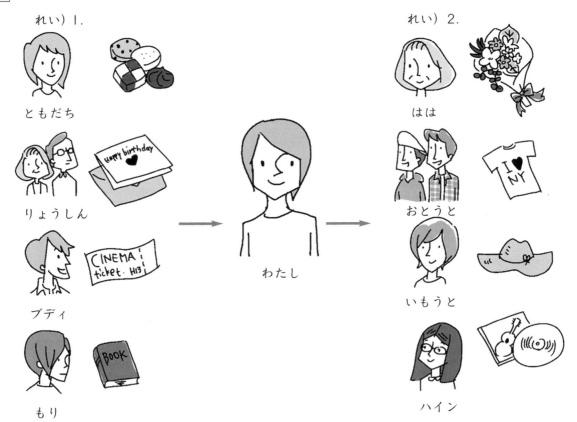

れい) 1. <u>ともだち</u>に <u>おかし</u>を もらいました。
れい) 2. <u>はは</u>に <u>はな</u>を あげました。

Structural Exercises : oral

e.g.) 1. Kono ryoori wa totemo <u>sukunai</u> desu.
       2. Kono ryoori wa totemo <u>sukunakatta</u> desu.

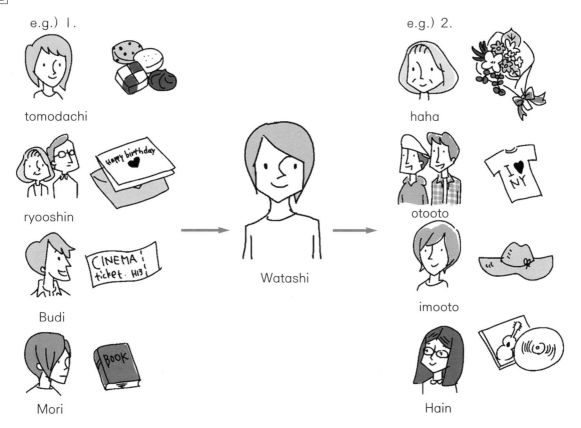

e.g.) 1. <u>Tomodachi</u> ni <u>okashi</u> o moraimashita.
e.g.) 2. <u>Haha</u> ni <u>hana</u> o agemashita.

3　わたしの　スケジュール

にちようび	げつようび	かようび	すいようび	もくようび	きんようび	どようび
わたし → はは			わたし → いもうと		ちち → わたし	ともだち → わたし

れい）　にちようびに　ははに　でんわします。

4　れい）　Ａ：①おかあさんは　どんな　②ひとですか。
　　　　　　　Ｂ：③しんせつな　ひとです。

1)　①せんせい　　　　②ひと　　　　③きびしい
2)　①インドネシア　　②ところ　　　③きれい
3)　①タイ　　　　　　②ところ　　　③たべものが　おいしい

3 Watashi no sukejuuru

nichi-yoobi	getsu-yoobi	ka-yoobi	sui-yoobi	moku-yoobi	kin-yoobi	do-yoobi
watashi ↓ haha 📱			watashi ↓ imooto 📱		chichi ↓ watashi 📱	tomodachi ↓ watashi ✉

e.g.) <u>Nichi-yoobi</u> ni <u>haha</u> ni <u>den'washimasu.</u>

4 e.g.) A：①<u>Okaa-san</u> wa don'na ②<u>hito</u> desu ka.

B：③<u>Shin'setsuna hito</u> desu.

1) ① sen'see   ② hito   ③ kibishii
2) ① In'doneshia   ② tokoro   ③ kiree
3) ① Tai   ② tokoro   ③ tabemono ga oishii

Conversational Exercises :

1. たかはし：それ、いいですね。

㉟　ブディ　：これですか。この　①とけいは　たんじょうびに
　　　　　　　②ともだちに　もらいました。

　　たかはし：へえ、いいですね。

1) ①にんぎょう　　　②せんぱい
2) ①Tシャツ　　　　②はは

2. せんせい：じゃ、きょうは　おわりましょう。

㊱　　　　　らいしゅうの　①ゼミは　②3じからです。

　　　　　　チンさん、③ブディさんに　でんわを　おねがいします。

　　チン　　：はい、わかりました。③ブディさんに　でんわします。

1) ①はっぴょう　　　②9じから　　　　③ハインさん
2) ①じゅぎょう　　　②やすみ　　　　　③アンさん

3. もり：アンさん、もうすぐ　ふゆやすみですね。

㊲　アン：そうですね。なにを　しますか。

　　もり：①おきなわに　いきます。

　　アン：①おきなわは　どんな　ところですか。

　　もり：②あたたかい　ところです。そして、③うみが　きれいです。

　　アン：そうですか。$\left\{\begin{array}{l}\text{いいですね。}\\\text{すごいですね。}\end{array}\right.$

1) ①おおさか　　　　②にぎやか　　　③たこやきが　おいしい
2) ①ほっかいどう　　②さむい　　　　③ゆきが　おおい

— 110 —

Conversational Exercises :

1. Takahashi：Sore, ii desu ne.

㉟　Budi　　：Kore desuka. Kono ① <u>tokee</u> wa tan'joobi ni
②<u>tomodachi</u> ni moraimashita.

Takahashi：Hee, ii desu ne.

1)　① nin'gyoo　　② sen'pai

2)　① T-shatsu　　② haha

2. sen'see：Ja, kyoo wa owarimashoo.

㊱　　　　　Rai-shuu no ①<u>zemi</u> wa ②<u>3-ji kara</u> desu.

Chin-san, ③<u>Budi-san</u> ni den'wa o onegaishimasu.

Chin　：Hai, wakarimashita.　③<u>Budi-san</u> ni den'washimasu.

1)　① happyoo　　② 9-ji kara　　③ Hain-san

2)　① jugyoo　　　② yasumi　　　③ An-san

3. Mori：An-san, moosugu fuyu-yasumi desu ne.

㊲　An　：Soo desu ne.　Nani o shimasu ka.

Mori：①<u>Okinawa ni</u> ikimasu.

An　：①<u>Okinawa</u> wa don'na tokoro desu ka.

Mori：②<u>Atatakai</u> tokoro desu.　Soshite, ③<u>umi ga kiree</u> desu.

An　：Soo desu ka.　{ Ii desune.
　　　　　　　　　　　Sugoi desune.

1)　① Oosaka　　② nigiyaka　　③ takoyaki ga oishii

2)　① Hokkaidoo　② samui　　　③ yuki ga ooi

— 111 —

4.
㊳
わたしの かぞくは 5にんです。
りょうしんと ①あねと あにが います。
②あねは かいしゃいんです。 ③とうきょうに います。
④あには きょうしです。⑤おおさかに います。

れい)　　　　　　　　　1)　　　　　　　　　2)

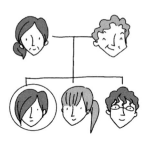

①あね / あに　　　　　①おとうと / いもうと　　①いもうと / あね
②かいしゃいん　　　　②だいがくせい　　　　　②こうこうせい
③とうきょう　　　　　③なごや　　　　　　　　③きょうと
④きょうし　　　　　　④だいがくいんせい　　　④いしゃ
⑤おおさか　　　　　　⑤ほっかいどう　　　　　⑤とうきょう

5.
㊴
ハイン：きょうは ①さむいですね。
ミン　：あした ②とうきょうに いきます。
　　　　てんきは どうですか。
ハイン：ちょっと しらべます。てんきよほうは・・・。
　　　　あ、あしたは ③はれです。
ミン　：そうですか。ありがとうございます。

1) ①あたたかい　②ほっかいどう　③ゆき
2) ①すずしい　　②おおさか　　　③あめ

— 112 —

4. Watashi no kazoku wa 5-nin desu.
Ryooshin to ①ane to ani ga imasu.
②Ane wa kaishain desu. ③Tookyoo ni imasu.
④Ani wa kyooshi desu. ⑤Oosaka ni imasu.

e.g.)

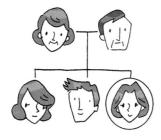

① ane / ani
② kaishain
③ Tookyoo
④ kyooshi
⑤ Oosaka

1)

① otooto / imooto
② daigakusee
③ Nagoya
④ daigakuin'see
⑤ Hokkaidoo

2)

① imooto / ane
② kookoosee
③ Kyooto
④ isha
⑤ Tookyoo

5.
Hain : Kyoo wa ①samui desu ne.
Minh : Ashita ②Tookyoo ni ikimasu.
　　　　Ten'ki wa doo desu ka.
Hain : Chotto shirabemasu. Ten'kiyohoo wa….
　　　　A ashita wa ③hare desu.
Minh : Soo desu ka. Arigatoo gozaimasu.

1) ① atatakai　　② Hokkaidoo　　③ yuki
2) ① suzushii　　② Oosaka　　③ ame

Structural Exercices : writing

1. 1) 【 にぎやかな ・ とうきょう ・ です ・ ところ ・ は 】

→_____

2) 【 4にん ・ わたし ・ は ・ です ・ の ・ かぞく 】

→_____

3) 【 は ・ ほっかいどう ・ います ・ に ・ はは 】

→_____

4) 【 あに ・ やさしい ・ です ・ ひと ・ は 】

→_____

5) 【 は ・ この ・ もらいました ・ に ・ ともだち ・ かばん 】

→_____

2. 1) へやに　パソコンが 【 います ・ あります 】。

2) あそこに　いぬが 【 います ・ あります 】。

3) コンビニは　あの　ビルの　1かいに 【 います ・ あります 】。

4) A：チンさんは　どこに 【 います ・ あります 】か。

B：チンさんですか。りょうに 【 います ・ あります 】。

5) ともだち 【 を ・ に 】 てがみ 【 を ・ に 】 かきました。

6) としょかん 【 に ・ で 】 ほん 【 を ・ に 】 かりました。

7) せんぱい 【 に ・ で 】 CD 【 を ・ に 】 かしました。

3. れい）おおさかは （ にぎやか<u>な</u> ） ところです。

ゆうめい ・ ~~にぎやか~~ ・ たかい ・ いそがしい ・ さむい ・ げんき

1) きょうは _____ です。あさから　ばんまで　じっけんです。

2) にほんは　5がつから　8がつまで　あついです。

12がつから　2がつまで _____ です。

3) 「あさくさ」は _____ かんこうちです。

4) あの　ひとは　とても　せが _____ です。190cmです。

5) もりさんは _____ ひとです。

— 114 —

Structural Exercices : writing

1. 1) 【 nigiyakana・Tookyoo・desu・tokoro・wa 】

→＿＿＿＿＿＿＿＿＿＿＿＿＿＿＿＿＿＿＿＿＿

2) 【 4-nin・watashi・wa・desu・no・kazoku 】

→＿＿＿＿＿＿＿＿＿＿＿＿＿＿＿＿＿＿＿＿＿

3) 【 wa・Hokkaidoo・imasu・ni・haha 】

→＿＿＿＿＿＿＿＿＿＿＿＿＿＿＿＿＿＿＿＿＿

4) 【 ani・yasashii・desu・hito・wa 】

→＿＿＿＿＿＿＿＿＿＿＿＿＿＿＿＿＿＿＿＿＿

5) 【 wa・kono・moraimashita・ni・tomodachi・kaban 】

→＿＿＿＿＿＿＿＿＿＿＿＿＿＿＿＿＿＿＿＿＿

2. 1) Heya ni pasokon ga 【 imasu・arimasu 】.

2) Asoko ni inu ga 【 imasu・arimasu 】.

3) Kon'bini wa ano biru no 1-kkai ni 【 imasu・arimasu 】.

4) A：Chin-san wa doko ni 【 imasu・arimasu 】 ka.

B：Chin-san desu ka. Ryoo ni 【 imasu・arimasu 】.

5) Tomodachi 【 o・ni 】 tegami 【 o・ni 】 kakimashita.

6) Toshokan 【 ni・de 】 hon 【 o・ni 】 karimashita.

7) Sen'pai 【 ni・de 】 CD 【 o・ni 】 kashimashita.

3. e.g.) Oosaka wa (nigiyaka<u>na</u>) tokoro desu.

yuumee・~~nigiyaka~~・takai・isogashii・samui・gen'ki

1) Kyoo wa ＿＿＿＿＿＿＿＿＿＿＿ desu. Asa kara ban made jikken desu.

2) Nihon wa 5-gatsu kara 8-gatsu made atsui desu.

12-gatsu kara 2-gatsu made ＿＿＿＿＿＿＿＿＿＿＿ desu.

3) "Asakusa" wa ＿＿＿＿＿＿＿＿＿＿＿ kan'koochi desu.

4) Ano hito wa totemo se ga ＿＿＿＿＿＿＿＿＿＿＿ desu. 190cm desu.

5) Mori-san wa ＿＿＿＿＿＿＿＿＿＿＿ hito desu.

4. 1) 【りょうしん ・ がくせい ・ なんにん ・ とうきょう】

A：Bさんの　かぞくは ＿＿＿＿＿＿＿＿＿＿　ですか。

B：5にんです。＿＿＿＿＿＿＿＿＿＿　と　あにと　おとうとが　います。

あには ＿＿＿＿＿＿＿＿＿＿　に　います。かいしゃいんです。

おとうとは ＿＿＿＿＿＿＿＿＿＿　です。おおさかに　います。

2) 【つま ・ ふたり ・ かいしゃいん】

わたしの　かぞくは ＿＿＿＿＿＿＿＿＿＿　です。

＿＿＿＿＿＿＿＿＿＿　が　います。

つまは ＿＿＿＿＿＿＿＿＿＿　です。

3) 【あたたかい ・ さむい ・ てんき ・ ゆき】

A：きょうは ＿＿＿＿＿＿＿＿＿＿　ですね。

あしたの ＿＿＿＿＿＿＿＿＿＿　は　どうですか。

B：＿＿＿＿＿＿＿＿＿＿　です。

A：えっ！じゃあ、＿＿＿＿＿＿＿＿＿＿　ですね。

4) 【でんわ ・ やすみ ・ わかりました】

A：らいしゅうの　じゅぎょうは＿＿＿＿＿＿＿＿＿＿　です。

Bさん、Cさんに＿＿＿＿＿＿＿＿＿＿　を　おねがいします。

B：＿＿＿＿＿＿＿＿＿＿　。でんわします。

5. れい）　A：きょうの　ごご　だれに　あいますか。【せんせい】

B：＿＿せんせいに　あいます。＿＿

1) A：だれに　その　プレゼントを　おくりますか。【ともだち】

B：＿＿＿＿＿＿＿＿＿＿＿＿＿＿＿＿＿＿＿＿＿＿＿＿＿＿

2) A：だれに　その　とけいを　もらいましたか。【こいびと】

B：＿＿＿＿＿＿＿＿＿＿＿＿＿＿＿＿＿＿＿＿＿＿＿＿＿＿

3) A：だれに　コンピューターの　ほんを　かりますか。【せんぱい】

B：＿＿＿＿＿＿＿＿＿＿＿＿＿＿＿＿＿＿＿＿＿＿＿＿＿＿

4. 1) 【 ryooshin ・ gakusee ・ nan-nin ・ Tookyoo 】

A : B-san no kazoku wa _____ desu ka.

B : 5-nin desu. _____ to ani to otooto ga imasu.

Ani wa _____ ni imasu. Kaishain desu.

Otooto wa _____ desu. Oosaka ni imasu.

2) 【 tsuma ・ futari ・ kaishain 】

Watashi no kazoku wa _____ desu.

_____ ga imasu.

Tsuma wa _____ desu.

3) 【 atatakai ・ samui ・ ten'ki ・ yuki 】

A : Kyoo wa _____ desu ne.

Ashita no _____ wa doo desu ka.

B : _____ desu.

A : Eh！ Jaa, _____ desu ne.

4) 【 den'wa ・ yasumi ・ wakarimashita 】

A : Rai-shuu no jugyoo wa _____ desu.

B-san, C-san ni _____ o onegaishimasu.

B : _____ . Den'washimasu.

5. e.g.)　　A : Kyoo no gogo dare ni aimasu ka. 【 sen'see 】

B : 　Sen'see ni aimasu.　

1) A : Dare ni sono purezen'to o okurimasu ka. 【 tomodachi 】

B : _____

2) A : Dare ni sono tokee o moraimashita ka. 【 koibito 】

B : _____

3) A : Dare ni kon'pyuutaa no hon o karimasu ka. 【 sen'pai 】

B : _____

— 117 —

6. しつもんに　こたえましょう。

1）（あなたの）ふるさとは　どんな　ところですか。

2）（あなたの）ふるさとは　なにが　ゆうめいですか。

3）にほんの　りょうりは　おいしいですか。なにが　おいしいですか。

4）にほんは　なにが　たかいですか。なにが　やすいですか。

5）いつも　だれに　メールしますか。

6）だれに　クリスマスプレゼントを　あげますか。

7）①たんじょうびに　なにを　もらいましたか。

　　②だれに　もらいましたか。

6. Shitsumon ni kotaemashoo.

1) (Anata no) furusato wa don'na tokoro desu ka.

2) (Anata no) furusato wa nani ga yuumee desu ka.

3) Nihon no ryoori wa oishii desu ka.　Nani ga oishii desu ka.

4) Nihon wa nani ga takai desu ka.　Nani ga yasui desu ka.

5) Itsumo dare ni meerushimasu ka.

6) Dare ni kurisumasu purezen'to o agemasu ka.

7) ①Tan'joobi ni nani o moraimashita ka.

　　②Dare ni moraimashita ka.

Activity 1   Let's go shopping!

★ Try to order and buy things at various shops and report the results.

Key Sentences

1. これは　なんですか。 Kore wa nan'desuka.

2. コーヒー　ふたつ、おねがいします。 Koohii futatsu onegaishimasu.

3. (ぜんぶで)　いくらですか。 (Zen'bu de) Ikura desuka.

Report :

どこで　[doko de]	なにを　[nani o]	いくら　[ikura]
e.g.) ばいてん [baiten]	コーヒー　ふたつ [koohii　futatsu]	280えん [280 en]

~~~~~~

Activity 2   Let's ask time!

★ Try to ask the information about time and report the answers.

Key Sentences

1. としょかんは　なんじから　なんじまでですか。 Toshokan wa nan'ji kara nan'ji made desuka.

2. やすみは　なんようびですか。 Yasumi wa nan'yoobi desuka.

Report :

どこ [doko]	なんじから　なんじまで [nan'ji kara nan'ji made]	やすみ [yasumi]
e.g.) としょかん [toshokan]	ごぜん9じから　　ごご6じまで [gozen 9ji kara gogo 6ji made]	にちようび [nichi-yoobi]

Lesson 1   Grammar Notes

《Typical Japanese Sentence Structures - 1-A》

Topic unit		Predicate (=Comment) unit		Question marker	
Noun 1 Noun phrase 1	は [wa]	Noun 2 Noun phrase 2	です[desu] では ありません / じゃ ありません [dewa' arimasen / ja' arimasen]	(か[ka])	。

《Typical Japanese Sentence Structures - 1-B》

Topic unit		Predicate (=Comment) unit		Question marker	
Noun 1 Noun phrase 1	も [mo]	Noun 2 Noun phrase 2	です[desu] では ありません / じゃ ありません [dewa' arimasen / ja' arimasen]	(か[ka])	。

《Typical Japanese Sentence Structures - 1-C》

Short answer		~~Topic unit~~		Predicate (=Comment) unit		
はい [hai] ええ [ee]	、	~~Noun 1~~ ~~Noun~~ ~~phrase 1~~	~~は [wa]~~ ~~も [mo]~~	Noun 2 Noun phrase 2 そう [soo]	です[desu]<hr>では ありません / じゃ ありません [dewa' arimasen / ja' arimasen]	。
いいえ [iie] いえ [ie]						
		ちがいます [chigaimasu]				

1.   Particles and their Position

Particles in Japanese serve a similar purpose to prepositions in English. We place prepositions before a noun in English but particles after a noun in Japanese. In this respect, particles are 'postpositions'. For example, with 'せん もん は[sen'mon wa]', the は[wa] is a particle and together with the preceding noun せん もん [sen'mon], makes one unit.

Particles have many different functions and meanings. Some of them act just as

— 121 —

markers without meanings such as a subject marker and a question marker. There is no English translation for them because English does not have prepositions to mark a subject or a question.

Other particles such as 'of', 'in', 'on', 'at', 'to', and 'from' have meanings. For example, with 'にほんの[nihon no]', the の[no] is a particle and together with the preceding noun にほん[nihon], makes one unit which means 'of Japan'.

2. Predicate Units and their Position

Predicates are a word group that explains the action, state, nature and such of the subject to complete the meaning of the sentence. In Japanese, there are three different types of predicate units; a regular verb alone; い [i] adjective alone; and 'Noun + です [desu]' combination (e.g. コンピューターです [kon'pyuutaa desu]). です [desu] is not a regular verb but an auxiliary verb, which always accompanies a noun. In this lesson, we will study 'Noun + です[desu]' predicate. い[i] adjectives will be introduced in Lesson 3. In Japanese, the predicate unit comes at the end of the sentence. That means we cannot tell if the sentence is either affirmative or negative until the end of the sentence in Japanese.

In English, depending on the subject, we must use the proper verb form. Namely, when the subject is 'I', the verb should be 'am' and 'you' requires 'are'. 'He / she / it' takes 'is'. However, in Japanese, regardless the subject, です[desu] does not change its form.

3. Topic Units

Japanese is a 'topic-comment language', while English is a 'subject-predicate language'. While regular English sentences must have a subject, Japanese sentences often lack a subject. It does not mean Japanese sentences do not require a subject but when the context can clarify what the subject is, we rather skip it. Often we can guess the subject from the topic but it is important to remember that a topic and a subject are different essentially. Sometimes a topic and a subject happen to be the same but not always. The topic of the sentence is about what the speaker makes comment later. We introduce the topic first to prepare listeners and then present a comment about the topic. The topic unit is 'Noun + は[wa]' and is placed at the beginning of the sentence. 'は' is normally pronounced *ha* but is *wa* when used as a particle.

① わたしは　がくせいです。
[watashi wa gakusee desu.]
I am a student. (Lit.: As for me, (I) am a student.)

② せんもんは　コンピューターです。
[sen'mon wa kon'pyuutaa desu.]
My major is computers. (Lit.: As for (my) major, (it) is computers.)

— 122 —

4. **Negative Form of です [desu]**

   Negative form of です [desu] is ではありません [dewa'arimasen]. Regardless the subject, the form is always the same. Its short form is じゃありません [ja'arimasen] and is a little less polite. The difference between the two is just like the one between 'is not' and 'isn't'. This book fucuses on conversation so we use じゃありません [ja'arimasen] here.

   ③ せんもんは　コンピューターでは　ありません。
   [sen'mon wa kon'pyuutaa dewa'arimasen.]
   My major is not computers.

   ④ せんもんは　コンピューターじゃ　ありません。
   [sen'mon wa kon'pyuutaa ja'arimasen.]
   My major isn't computers.

5. **Also : Noun + も [mo] / Noun 1 + も [mo] + Noun 2 + も [mo]**

   も [mo] as a particle means 'also'. For example, 'ハインさんも [Hain-san mo]' means 'Hien also'. 'Noun 1 + も [mo] + Noun 2 + も [mo]' means, 'both Noun 1 and Noun 2'.

   ⑤ ブディさんは　がくせいです。ハインさんも　がくせいです。
   [Budi-san wa gakusee desu.　Hain-san mo gakusee desu.]
   Budhi is a student. Hien also is a student.

   ⑥ ブディさんも　ハインさんも　がくせいです。
   [Budi-san mo Hain-san mo gakusee desu.]
   Both Budhi and Hien are students.

6. **Questions - 1: Yes/No Question**

   There are 2 types of questions; 'Yes/No question', which requires an affirmative or a negative answer and 'Interrogative question'. In order to produce Yes/No question in English, we have to change word order around, besides adding a question marker at the end of the sentence. Check the following example ⑦.

   ⑦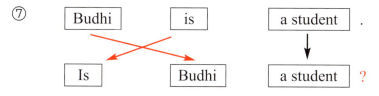

   It is much easier to make Yes/No question in Japanese. By simply adding a question marker か [ka] at the end of the sentence, we can produce Yes/No question as follows. We do not have to change anything else.

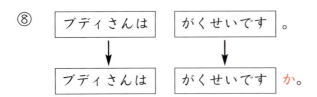

[Budi-san wa gakusee desu.]
Budhi is a student.

[Budi-san wa gakusee desu ka.]
Is Budhi a student?

7. **Simple Answers : はい [hai] & いいえ [iie]**

In order to answer Yes/No question affirmatively, we say はい [hai] which means 'Yes'; on the other hand, when answering negatively, we say いいえ [iie] which means 'No'. Their short forms are ええ [ee] and いえ [ie] respectively. Usually the short forms are less polite than their full-length forms but ええ [ee] and いえ [ie] are not that case. They sound a little less decisively and convey a slight hesitation of the speaker. ええ [ee] is also used by the listener to let the speaker know that the listener is listening. In that case, ええ [ee] does not necessarily mean that the listener agrees with the speaker.

8. **そうです [soo desu]**

The word そう [soo] is a noun and often used to answer Yes/No question. When answering affirmatively, we say そうです [soo desu] ; on the other hand, when answering negatively, either そうじゃ ありません [soo ja'arimasen] or ちがいます [chigaimasu] can be used. そうじゃ ありません [soo ja'arimasen] means 'It is not so' and ちがいます [chigaimasu] means 'It is wrong. (Lit.: It is different from what you thought.)'

Also the expression そうですか [soo desu ka] is used to acknowledge new information. We pronounce it with a flat intonation. (The red arrow in example ⑨ shows the intonation.)

⑨ あ、そうですか。[a, soo desu ka. →] Well, is that so?

9. **How to Connect 2 Nouns - 1**

Two nouns may be connected by の [no] to make a noun phrase which acts as a noun. In 'Noun 1 + の [no] + Noun 2' structure, Noun 1 represents an organisation / group / owner to which Noun 2 belongs. We will study this more in Lesson 2.

⑩ わたしは あおぞらだいがくの がくせいです。
[watashi wa aozora daigaku no gakusee desu.]
I'm a student of Aozora University.

10. Saying Where You Are from

In order to tell someone where you are from (typically when introducing yourself), we can use the structure 'place + から　きました [kara kimashita]'. Here から[kara] is a particle which means 'from' and きました [kimashita] is a regular verb which means 'came'. There is more information about regular verbs in Lesson 6 but until then, we treat this structure as an idiom.

⑪　わたしは　マレーシアから　きました。
[watashi wa mareeshia kara kimashita.]
I came from Malaysia.

11. Concept of Units

In Japanese, the concept of units is important. In English, we may change 'word order'; however, in Japanese, we may change 'unit order' instead. Units can be made in many different ways : typical examples are 'Noun / Noun phrase + particle' combination, 'Noun / Noun phrase + です[desu]' combination, and regular verb alone.

12. Elimination of Information

In Japanese, once we register any information into the conversation and share it between the speaker and the listeners, we can skip that information. We can register information in many different ways such as by statement or by gesture. In the following conversation, nouns わたし[watashi] and せんもん[sen'mon] are eliminated when they appear for the second time. Make sure to eliminate the information by units not by words.

⑫　ブディ：わたしは　ブディです。（わたしは）がくせいです。
[Budi　: watashi wa Budi desu. (watashi wa) gakusee desu.]
Budhi　: I am Budhi. (I am) a student.

せんもんは　コンピューターです。
[sen'mon wa kon'pyuutaa desu.]
(My) major is computers.

ハイン：わたしも（せんもんは）コンピューターです。
[Hain　: watashi mo (sen'mon wa) kon'pyuutaa desu.]
Hien　: My (major) also is computers.

Lesson 2　Grammar Notes

《Demonstratives - 1》

Noun / Noun phrase		Meaning	
これ [kore]	this one	Refers to something near the speaker	
この [kono] + Noun 1	this Noun 1		
それ [sore]	that one	Refers to something near the listener	
その [sono] + Noun 1	that Noun 1		
あれ [are]	that one over there	Refers to something far from both the speaker and the listener	
あの [ano] + Noun 1	that Noun 1 over there		
どれ [dore]	which one	Asking to specify one out of many choices	
どの [dono] + Noun 1	which Noun 1		

《Typical Japanese Sentence Structures - 2》

Meaning	Predicate (= Comment) unit					Question marker	
	Noun phrase						
	Modifier		Modified noun				
	Noun	Interrogative counterpart					
Organization	あおぞらだいがく [aozora daigaku]	*どこ [doko]		がくせい [gakusee]			
Field / category	コンピューター [kon'pyuutaa]	なん [nan]		ざっし [zasshi]			
Ownership	わたし [watashi]	だれ [dare]		かさ [kasa]			
	ハインさん [Hain-san]	**どなた [donata]	の	ほん [hon]	です [desu]	(か [ka])	。
Manufacturer	アッパル [apparu]	*どこ [doko]		パソコン [pasokon]			
Producing area	アメリカ [amerika]	*どこ [doko]		しんぶん [shin'bun]			
Seller, dealer	としょかん [toshokan]	*どこ [doko]		ほん [hon]			
				の ⇒ φ [no]			

* どこ [doko] means 'where' or 'which place' and will be introduced in Lesson 5.
** どなた [donata] is an honorific counterpart of だれ [dare].

— 126 —

1. **Demonstratives - 1**

   Demonstratives ; これ [kore], それ [sore], あれ [are], and どれ [dore] are all nouns by themselves and are followed by a particle directly. On the other hand, この [kono], その [sono], あの [ano], and どの [dono] cannot be used alone ; they must be accompanied by a noun to make a noun phrase. Once it becomes a noun phrase, a particle can follow it. While the space is divided into two ; here and there in English, it is divided into three in Japanese. こ [ko] series such as これ [kore] and この [kono] refers to something near the speaker ; そ [so] series such as それ [sore] and その [sono] refers to something near the listener ; あ [a] series such as あれ [are] and あの [ano] refers to something far from both the speaker and the listener. ど [do] series such as どれ [dore] and どの [dono] will be used to ask to specify one out of many choices. Demonstratives are called 'こそあど [ko-so-a-do] words' in Japanese taking the first letters of each word. In this lesson, we introduce two sets of them. これ [kore], それ [sore], あれ [are], and どれ [dore] cannot be used to refer to people.

2. **How to Connect 2 Nouns - 2**

   It was explained in Lesson 1 that の [no] is used to connect two nouns. In 'Noun 1 + の [no] + Noun 2' structure, Noun 1 modifies Noun 2 and they together make one phrase. It is often translated as 'of'. 'わたしの かさ [watashi no kasa]' means 'an umbrella of me (=my umbrella)' and 'トヨラの くるま [toyora no kuruma]' means 'a car of Toyora (=Toyora's car). の [no] can connect nouns that mean many different things. Refer to the chart in page 126 for some examples. Their interrogative counterparts (used in questions) are also listed.

3. **Pronoun の[no] and its Elimination**

   の[no] can be used as a noun to mean something like 'one'; therefore it can replace a regular noun where the context clarifies what the 'one' is. の[no] can replace things, but cannot not replace people. That is to say, 'アッパルの　パソコン[apparu no pa sokon]' can technically be rephrased as 'アッパルの　の[apparu no no]'. However, when two の[no] are side by side, the latter の[no] is omitted.

   アッパルの　パソコン [apparu no pasokon]
   An Apparu (company name)'s PC
   ⇨ アッパルの　の [apparu no no]
      An Apparu's one
      ⇨ アッパルの　の [apparu no no]
         An Apparu's one
         ⇨ アッパルの [apparu no]
            An Apparu's

4. **Questions – 2: Interrogative Questions**

   We use interrogative questions to ask to identify unknown information. We can make interrogative questions in Japanese by simply placing the proper interrogative word at where we normally place the answer. The word order is exactly same as regular sentences. The releationship between regular sentences and interrogative sentences is very clear as in the examples ① and ② below. Example ① literally means 'As for the major, it is Japanese' and ② means 'As for the major, what is it?'. Equally example ③ literally means 'As for this, it is an umbrella of me' and ④ means 'As for this, is it an umbrella of who?'.

   We cannot use an interrogative word in the topic, because we cannot make unknown information a topic. Example ⑤ literally means 'As for what, is it computers?' and it does not make any sense. It is important to remember that interrogative words and topic marker は[wa] do not go together.

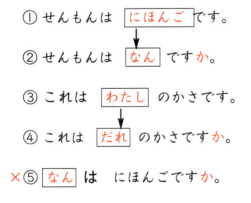

① せんもんは にほんご です。　　[sen'mon wa nihon'go desu.]
　　　　　　　　　　　　　　　　My major is Japanese.
② せんもんは なん ですか。　　　[sen'mon wa nan desu ka.]
　　　　　　　　　　　　　　　　What is your major?
③ これは わたし のかさです。　　[kore wa watashi no kasa desu.]
　　　　　　　　　　　　　　　　This is my umbrella.
④ これは だれ のかさですか。　　[kore wa dare no kasa desu ka.]
　　　　　　　　　　　　　　　　Whose umbrella is this?
×⑤ なん は にほんごですか。　　[nan wa nihon'go desu ka.]
　　　　　　　　　　　　　　　　× As for what, is it Japanese?
　　　　　　　　　　　　　　　　(×interrogative + **topic marker** は[wa])

5. How to Tell Your Nationality

It is easy to tell someone your nationality in Japanese. Just add じん [jin] right after the country name. To say 'Japanese citizen' we say 'にほん [nihon] + じん [jin]' and 'American citizen' is 'アメリカ [amerika] + じん [jin]'.

6. Sentence Ending Particles: ね[ne] & よ[yo]

ね [ne] and よ [yo] are sentence ending particles and are put at the end of a declarative sentence (a sentence that states or defines information).

ね [ne] makes a tag question. With a rising intonation, the speaker is attempting to get the listener to agree or confirm as in example ⑥, where the listener is expected to say yes or no in his/her reply. With a flat intonation, it makes the statement a little milder as in example ⑦, where the listener is not expected to say anything specific. This is an effective conversation technique and the same goes for English. (The red arrows below show the intonations.)

⑥ A : これは　にほんごの　ほんですね。↗　[kore wa nihongo no hon desu ne. ↗]
　　　　　　　　　　　　　　　　　　　This is a Japanese book, isn't it? ↗
　 B : はい、そうです。　　　　　　　 [hai, soo desu.]
　　　　　　　　　　　　　　　　　　　Yes, it is so.

⑦ A : これは　にほんごの　ほんですね。→　[kore wa nihongo no hon desu ne. →]
　　　　　　　　　　　　　　　　　　　This is a Japanese book, isn't it? →
　 B : そうですか。　　　　　　　　　 [soo desu ka.]
　　　　　　　　　　　　　　　　　　　Is that so?

よ [yo] is used when the speaker is trying to provide information which he/she believes the listener does not have. So if you use よ [yo] with the information the listener surely knows, it is strange. Example ⑧ literally means '(I believe you do not know it. So I will tell you.) You are a student'. This sentence is strange because we normally expect people know what they are. This sentence is only possible when the speaker tries to call the listner's attention to what he is. よ [yo] is pronounced always with a flat intonation. If you use よ [yo] too often, you could come across as being arrogant.

⑧ あなたは　がくせいですよ。　　　　 [anata wa gakusee desu yo.]
　　　　　　　　　　　　　　　　　　　You are a student, y'know.

— 129 —

Lesson 3 Grammar Notes

《**Adjectives as Predicates**》

Forms	い[i] adjectives (polite form)			な[na] adjectives (polite form)
	い[i] adjectives (plain form)		+Politeness marker	
	Regular い[i] adjectives	いい[ii] (Exception)		
Affirmative	～い [～i]	いい [ii]	+です [desu]	～です [～desu]
Negative	～くない [～kunai]	よくない [yokunai]		～じゃ ありません [～ja' arimasen]
Affirmative-Past	～かった [～katta]	よかった [yokatta]		～でした [～deshita]
Negative-Past	～くなかった [～kunakatta]	よくなかった [yokunakatta]		～じゃ ありませんでした [～ja' arimasen'deshita]

1. **Adjectives**

   Adjectives are used to indicate the state of a noun or to modify a noun. In Japanese, there are two different groups of adjectives; い[i] adjectives and な[na] adjectives. Both of them can be used either to modify a noun (examples ① and ②) or to complete a sentence as a predicate (examples ③ and ④). They are both adjectives semantically, but are conjugated differently.

2. **Adjectives to Modify Nouns**

   The names of い[i] adjectives and な[na] adjectives came from their forms when they modify nouns. When い[i] adjective modifies a noun, the last syllable of the adjective is い[i] as in example ①. When な[na] adjective modifies a noun, the last syllable of the adjective is な[na] as in example ②. In both cases, 'Adjective+Noun' combination makes a noun phrase and です[desu] is following the phrase. This です[desu] is a verb and can conjugate.

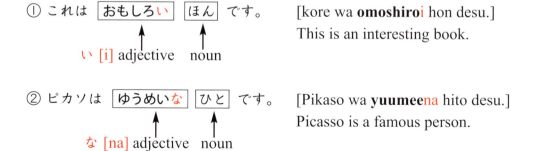

3. **い [i] adjectives as Predicates**

   い[i] adjectives have verb-function built in; that is, 'むずかしい[muzukashii]' is not just 'difficult' but '*is* difficult'. Outwardly 'にほんごは　むずかしい[nihongo wa muzukashii.]' seems to be incomplete but it is actually a complete sentence. です[desu] may follow い[i] adjectives as in example ③ but this です[desu] is not a verb and cannot conjugate. It is a politeness marker, which is an option to add politeness to the sentence. 'にほんごは　むずかしい[nihongo wa muzukashii.]' and 'にほんごは　むずかしいです[nihongo wa muzukashii desu.]' are exactly the same semantically and only the difference is their politeness. The former is a plain sentence without any politeness implied and the latter is a polite sentence. We use plain sentences in conversations with someone close to us such as friends and family members, to whom we do not have to be formal. On the other hand, polite sentences include the minimum level of politeness and we can use them at almost any situations safely.

   Because い[i] adjectives have verb-function built in, we can conjugate them directly. As you can see in the inflection chart in page 130, い[i] adjectives have their own affirmative, negative, past, and negative past forms. These forms are all plain but we can make them polite by adding the politeness marker です[desu] at the end. All い[i] adjectives follow the same inflection rules but we have one exception. いい[ii] conjugates differently as seen in the chart. Usually いい[ii] will be an only exception to い[i] adjectives with regard to their inflection.

   ③ にほんごは　むずかしい（です）。　　　[nihon-go wa muzukashii (desu).]
   　　　　　　　↑　　　　　　　　　　　　　Japanese is difficult.
   　　い [i] adjective as a predicate

4. **な [na] adjectives as Predicates**

   な[na] adjectives do not include verb-function and we cannot conjugate them. しんせつ[shin'setsu] means 'kind' and if you want to use it as a predicate, you must add 'is' which is です [desu] in Japanese as in example ④. This です[desu] is a verb, so we can conjugate it. In this respect, it is not wrong to say な[na] adjectives act similarly to nouns.

   ④ ブディさんは　しんせつです。　　　　[Budi-san wa shin'setsu desu.]
   　　　　　　　　　↑　　　　　　　　　　Budhi is kind.
   　　な [na] adjective as a predicate

5. **2 Kinds of です [desu]**

   です[desu] in example ③ is a politeness marker which is an option. However, です[desu] in examples ①, ②, and ④ are all verbs and, that is, they conjugate and are an essential component for sentences.

6. **Adjective Stems**

Adjective stems will be made by removing いです [idesu] from a polite い [i] adjective form or です [desu] from a polite な [na] adjective form. The stems do not function independently.

- い [i] adjectives : おいし~~いです~~   むずかし~~いです~~
  [oishi ~~idesu~~]   [muzukashi~~idesu~~]
- な [na] adjectives : きれい~~です~~   じょうず~~です~~
  [kiree ~~desu~~]   [joozu ~~desu~~]

7. **Adjective Stem + そうです [soo desu]**

When talking about your observations of something or someone, you can use 'Adjective stem + そうです [soo desu]'. This structure expresses your guess based on your visual observation only. If you have more information acquired in a different way such as hearing in rumors and reading articles, this structure cannot be used.

⑤ にほんごは　むずかし　そうです。　　（い [i] adjectives)

[nihon-go wa **muzukashi** soo desu.]

Japanese looks difficult.

⑥ あのひとは　しんせつ　そうです。　　（な [na] adjectives)

[ano hito wa **shinsetsu** soo desu.]

That person looks kind.

8. **Adjective Stem + すぎます [sugimasu]**

'Adjective stem + すぎます [sugimasu]' means that something is 'too much' or 'exessive'.

⑦ にほんごは　むずかし　すぎます。　　（い [i] adjectives)

[nihon-go wa **muzukashi** sugimasu.]

Japanese is too difficult.

⑧ にほんごの　べんきょうは　たいへん　すぎます。　　（な [na] adjectives)

[nihon-go no ben'kyoo wa **taihen** sugimasu.]

Studying Japanese is too hard.

9. **Questions – 3: Negative Questions**

We often use negative questions to confirm our concern or anxiety. We also use a negative question as an invitation, We will study this usage later.

⑨ このカレー、からく**ない**ですか。　　[kono karee, **karaku**nai desu ka.]

Isn't this curry hot?

ええ、からいです。　　[ee, karai desu]

Yes, it is hot.

— 132 —

⑩ えいごは　むずかしくないですか。　　[eego wa **muzukashiku**nai desu ka.]

Isn't Englsih difficult?

いいえ、むずかしくないです。　　[iie, muzukashikunai desu.]

No, it is not difficult.

10. Sentence Fillers

There are many types of filler in Japanese. In linguistics, filler is a sound or word used in conversation to let others know that he/she has paused to think, but he/she has not yet finished speaking. In English, for example, some of the most common filler sounds are 'uh' and 'er'. Young people often use words such as 'like', 'y'know', 'I mean', 'so', 'actually', and 'basically' as fillers. Below are some examples of Japanese fillers along with the lesson numbers in which they appear in this book.

あ [a] (L1,2,4,5,6,7,8,)　　ああ[aa] (L2,7)　　あの [ano] (L1,4,5,7,)
うーん [uun] (L3,6)　　えっ！？ [e] (L4,5,6,8)　　えーっと [eetto] (L4,5)
さあ [saa] (L3)　　へえ [hee] (L2,7,8)　　わあ [waa] (L3,5,6,7,8)

11. Refusing with Hesitation

When you want to refuse someone or something without hurting the listener's feelings or being a stick in the mud, you can use ちょっと．．．[chotto…] with a sustaining tone at the end. This expression cushions the answer, so make sure not to say a flat out いいえ[iie] together with this expression.

More often, we use a filler such as うーん[uun] or えーっと[eetto] first to suggest that you are having a difficult time making the decision.

⑪ A：わさびは　どうですか。　　[wasabi wa doo desu ka.]

How about wasabi?

B：うーん、ちょっと．．．。　　[uun, chotto… .]

Mmm, actually…(no).

— 133 —

Lesson 4   Grammar Notes

《Sino Japanese Counting System》

1	いち	[ichi]	400	よん　ひゃく	[yon hyaku]	
2	に	[ni]	500	ご　　ひゃく	[go hyaku]	
3	さん	[san]	600	ろっ　ぴゃく	[rop pyaku]	
4	し／よん	[shi / yon]	700	なな　ひゃく	[nana hyaku]	
5	ご	[go]	800	はっ　ぴゃく	[hap pyaku]	
6	ろく	[roku]	900	きゅうひゃく	[kyuu hyaku]	
7	しち／なな	[shichi / nana]	**1000**	φ　せん	**[sen]**	
8	はち	[hachi]	2000	に　　せん	[ni sen]	
9	きゅう	[kyuu]	3000	さん　ぜん	[san zen]	
10	じゅう	[juu]	4000	よん　せん	[yon sen]	
11	じゅう　いち	[juu ichi]	5000	ご　　せん	[go sen]	
14	じゅう　よん	[juu yon]	6000	ろく　せん	[roku sen]	
32	さんじゅう　に	[san'juu ni]	7000	なな　せん	[nana sen]	
56	ごじゅう　ろく	[gojuu roku]	8000	はっ　せん	[has sen]	
78	しちじゅう　はち／ななじゅう　はち [shichijuu hachi / nanajuu hachi]		9000	きゅうせん	[kyuu sen]	
99	きゅうじゅう　きゅう [kyuujuu kyuu]		**10000**	いち　まん	**[ichi man]**	
100	φ　ひゃく	**[hyaku]**	33300	さんまん　さんぜん　さんびゃく [san'man san'zen san'byaku]		
143	ひゃく　よんじゅう　さん [hyaku yon'juu san]		48600	よんまん　はっせん　ろっぴゃく [yon'man hassen roppyaku]		
200	に　　ひゃく	[ni hyaku]	72800	ななまん　にせん　はっぴゃく [nanaman nisen happyaku]		
300	さん　びゃく	[san byaku]	91010	きゅうまん　せん　じゅう [kyuuman sen jyuu]		

《Japanese Original Counting System》

1	ひとつ	[hitotsu]	7	ななつ	[nanatsu]
2	ふたつ	[futatsu]	8	やっつ	[yattsu]
3	みっつ	[mittsu]	9	ここのつ	[kokonotsu]
4	よっつ	[yottsu]	10	とお	[too]
5	いつつ	[itsutsu]	?	いくつ	[ikutsu]
6	むっつ	[muttsu]			

1. Numbers

There are two different counting systems in Japanese: one is originally Japanese and the other is Chinese origin. While the Japanese original system has only from one to ten, the Sino system has zero to infinity. Red color in the chart shows exceptions to pronunciation.

Japanese counting system is easy if you put comma after every four digits. Every comma has its name and the first comma's name is まん[man]. For example, 25,252,525 can be analysed as in the chart below and we read it as 'にせん　ごひゃく　にじゅう　ご まん　にせん　ごひゃく　にじゅう　ご [nisen gohyaku nijuu go man nisen gohyaku nijuu go]'. Obviously 'にせん　ごひゃく　にじゅう　ご [nisen gohyaku nijuu go]' is repeated with まん[man] in-between. That means as far as you remember how to read four digits' numbers and the names for each comma, you can read infinite number in Japanese.

2	×1000	5	×100	2	×10	5	,	2	×1000	5	×100	2	×10	5
に	せん	ご	ひゃく	に	じゅう	ご	まん	に	せん	ご	ひゃく	に	じゅう	ご

2. Counters

Unlike in English, numbers cannot modify nouns directly in Japanese. Therefore 'number + noun' combination does not exist in Japanese. 'Two computers' is not '2 (= に) コンピューター [ni kon'pyuutaa]' or 'ふたつ　コンピューター[futatsu kon'pyuu taa]. That means we cannot simply say, 'I have two computers' in Japanese. Instead, to

— 135 —

express the same situation, we have to say something like, 'I have computers to the amount of two'.

In Japanese, counters usually accompany numbers and they make adverbs together. There are many counters in Japanese for specific items; for example, Japanese currency Yen is also a counter. 'Number + counter' combination is called 'quantifier'.

However, the Japanese original counting system does not require any counter and we use it for counting small items that do not have proper counters. That means the Japanese original system has the counter function already built in.

The Sino system is normally accomnaied by counters but when counting more than ten items that do not have proper counters, we use the Sino system without any counters.

3. **How to Connect 2 Nouns - 3**

We introduced the particle の[no] to connect two nouns in Lessons 1 and 2. There are several other particles as well to connect two nouns such as と[to] and や[ya]. Whileの [no] in 'Noun 1+の[no]+Noun 2' is used to show an organisation/group/owner to which Noun 2 belongs, と[to] simply connects two nouns equally and 'Noun 1 + と[to] + Noun 2' means 'Noun 1 and Noun 2' simply. や[ya] also connects two nouns but it means 'Noun 1 and Noun 2 and others'. Both make a noun phrase that can act as a noun. We will study や[ya] in Lesson 9 again.

① どようびと　にちようびは　やすみです。
　　[do-yoobi to nichi-yoobi wa yasumi desu.]
　　I have a day off on Saturday and Sunday.
② おにぎりや　ラーメンは　おいしいです。
　　[onigiri ya raamen wa oishii desu.]
　　Onigiri and ramen (and other foods) are delicious.

4. **Ordering Foods**

You can order foods at a restaurant using a noun and quantifier with ください [kudasai] or おねがいします [onegaishimasu] at the end of the sentence as follows. You may switch the orders of a noun and a quantifier but normally we tell a noun first.

③ ハンバーガー、ふたつ　ください。　　　[han'baagaa, futatsu kudasai.]
　　　　　　　　　　　　　　　　　　　　Two hamburgers, please.

④ おにぎり、みっつ　おねがいします。　　[onigiri, mittsu onegaishimasu.]
　　　　　　　　　　　　　　　　　　　　Three onigiri, please.

— 136 —

Lesson 5　Grammar Notes

《Tense》

Predicate		Non-past (future / present)	Past
Noun + です [desu]	Affirmative	Noun + です [desu]	Noun + でした　　[deshita]
	Negative	Noun + じゃ　ありません [ja' arimasen]	Noun + じゃ　ありませんでした [ja' arimasen'deshita]
Regular verb	Affirmative	〜ます　　　[〜masu] (eg. みます　[mimasu])	〜ました　　　[〜mashita] (eg. みました　[mimashita])
	Negative	〜ません　　[〜masu] (eg. みません [mimasen])	〜ませんでした　[〜masen'deshita] (eg. みませんでした [mimasen'deshita])

《Time Expressions – 1: Point in Time》

AM	ごぜん [gozen]	PM	ごご [gogo]

Suffix	o'clock （〜じ [ji]）		Minutes （〜ふん [fun] / ぷん [pun]）	
1	いち	じ [ichi - ji]	いっ　　　　　ぷん	[ip - pun]
2	に	じ [ni - ji]	に　　　　　ふん	[ni - fun]
3	さん	じ [san - ji]	さん　　　　ぷん	[san - pun]
4	よ	じ [yo - ji]	よん　　　　ぷん	[yon - pun]
5	ご	じ [go - ji]	ご　　　　　ふん	[go - fun]
6	ろく	じ [roku - ji]	ろっ　　　　ぷん	[rop - pun]
7	しち	じ [shichi - ji]	しち　　　　ふん	[shichi - fun]
8	はち	じ [hachi - ji]	はっぷん / はち　ふん	[hap - pun / hachi - fun]
9	く	じ [ku - ji]	きゅう　　　ふん	[kyuu - fun]
10	じゅう	じ [juu - ji]	じゅっ　　　ぷん	[jup - pun]
11	じゅう　いち	じ [juu ichi - ji]	じゅう　いっ　ぷん	[juu ip - pun]
12	じゅう　に	じ [juu ni - ji]	じゅう　に　ふん	[juu ni - fun]
24	にじゅう　よ	じ [nijuu yo - ji]	にじゅう　よん　ぷん	[nijuu yon - pun]
?	なん	じ [nan - ji]	なん　　　　ぷん	[nan - pun]

— 137 —

《Time Expressions – 2 : Duration》

	Days	Weeks	Months	Years
1	いちにち [ichi - nichi]	いっしゅうかん [is -shuukan]	いっかげつ [ik - kagetsu]	いちねん [ichi - nen]
2	ふつか [futsuka]	にしゅうかん [ni - shuukan]	にかげつ [ni - kagetsu]	にねん [ni - nen]
3	みっか [mikka]	さんしゅうかん [san - shuukan]	さんかげつ [san - kagetsu]	さんねん [san - nen]
4	よっか [yokka]	よんしゅうかん [yon - shuukan]	よんかげつ [yon - kagetsu]	よねん [yo - nen]
5	いつか [itsuka]	ごしゅうかん [go - shuukan]	ごかげつ [go - kagetsu]	ごねん [go - nen]
6	むいか [muika]	ろくしゅうかん [roku - shuukan]	ろっかげつ [rok - kagetsu]	ろくねん [roku - nen]
7	なのか [nanoka]	ななしゅうかん [nana - shuukan]	ななかげつ [nana - kagetsu]	しち／ななねん [shichi / nana - nen]
8	ようか [yooka]	はっしゅうかん [has - shuukan]	はちかげつ [hachi - kagetsu]	はちねん [hachi - nen]
9	ここのか [kokonoka]	きゅうしゅうかん [kyuu - shuukan]	きゅうかげつ [kyuu - kagetsu]	きゅうねん [kyuu - nen]
10	とおか [tooka]	じゅっしゅうかん [jus - shuukan]	じゅっかげつ [juk -kagetsu]	じゅうねん [jyuu - nen]
?	なんにち [nan - nichi]	なんしゅうかん [nan - shuukan]	なんかげつ [nan - kagetsu]	なんねん [nan - nen]

《Time Expressions – 3 : Frequency & Adverbs for Days》

Prefix / Suffix	every	last	this / now	next
day	まいにち [mai - nichi]	*きのう [kinoo]	*きょう [kyoo]	*あした [ashita]
week	まいしゅう [mai - shuu]	せんしゅう [sen - shuu]	こんしゅう [kon - shuu]	らいしゅう [rai - shuu]
month	まいつき [mai - tsuki]	せんげつ [sen - getsu]	こんげつ [kon - getsu]	らいげつ [rai - getsu]
year	まいねん／まいとし [mai - nen / mai - toshi]	きょねん [kyo - nen]	ことし [kotoshi]	らいねん [rai - nen]
morning	まいあさ [mai - asa]		けさ [kesa]	
evening	まいばん [mai - ban]		*こんばん [kon - ban]	

* きのう [kinoo] is not 'last day' but 'yesterday' and *あした [ashita] is 'tomorrow' not 'next day'.
Also *きょう [kyoo] is not 'this day' but 'today' and   *こんばん [kon'ban] is tonight not 'this night'.
Others are the combinations of the regular prefix and suffix like 'まいにち[mai-nichi] = every + day'.

《**Demonstratives – 2**》

Noun		Meaning	
ここ	[koko]	this place	Refers to where the speaker is
こちら	[kochira]	this place (polite) this direction	
そこ	[soko]	that place	Refers to where the listener is
そちら	[sochira]	that place (polite) that direction	
あそこ	[asoko]	that place over there	Refers to somewhere far from both the speaker and the listener
あちら	[achira]	that place over there (polite) that direction over there	
どこ	[doko]	which place	Asking which place or direction
どちら	[dochira]	which place (polite) which direction	

1. Tense

Japanese has only two tenses; 'non-past' and past. The non-past tense covers both present and future. It also shows a habitual event or a truth.

As we studied in Lesson 1, in Japanese, there are three different types of predicate units; a regular verb alone; い [i] adjective alone; 'Noun + です [desu]' combination. All of them have their non-past and past forms and each tense has both affirmative and negative forms; that means all predicates have four different forms. The chart 'Tense' in page 137 shows the inflections of the auxiliary verb です [desu] and regular verbs. All regular verbs end with ます [masu] in polite form. Therefore polite form is also called ます [masu] form. The conjugations in ます [masu] form are quite simple without any exception as shown in the chart.

You may distinguish future and present by the context, which becomes often obvious with time expressions such as 'today' or 'tomorrow'.

① テストは　あした　おわります。　[tesuto wa ashita owarimasu.]
　　　　　　　　　　　　　　　　　　The test will finish tomorrow.

② きょうは　6 じに　おきました。　[kyoo wa roku-ji ni okimashita.]
　　　　　　　　　　　　　　　　　　I woke up at 6 o'clock today.

— 139 —

2. Time Expressions - 1

The charts in pages 137 and 138 show some of the time expressions often used in our daily lives. The suffix for hours is ' じ [ji]' and the one for minites is ' ふん [fun]'. じ [ji] does not change the form regardless the number but ふん [fun] changes its form depending on the number that ふん [fun] accompanies as in 'Time Expressions 1 – Point in Time' in page 137, where the irregular pronunciations are marked by bold; besides red color shows regular suffixes.

In Japanese, we place the words for time in order of sizes of their concepts. For example, conceptwise, years are bigger than months, and hours are bigger than minutes. When reading a calender, year comes first and month and day will follow in this order. When reading a clock, after a.m. or p.m., hour, minute and second will follow in this order.

This thought orientation is true with the words for space. The address in Japanese starts with its prefecture (something like states or provinces). City, street name, house number, and room number will follow in this order.

  ③ ごぜん　9じ　7ふん　です。 [gozen ku-ji nana-fun desu.]
              It is 7 minutes past 9 o'clock a.m.

3. Particles for Time Expressions

Time expressions in 'Time Expressions 1 – Point in Time' in page 137 are all nouns, which show the names of points in time, not the duration of time. Depending on what you want to say, you must use proper particles with those nouns. They together make an adverbial phrase unit, which modifies a predicate as seen in the chart below. These particles are examples of those for time, but we can also use them for space. We will cover this usage for space in Lesson 6.

On the other hand, time expressions in 'Time Expressions 2 and 3' in page 138 are all adverbs alone and do not take particles. We can use them directly to modify a predicate. In these charts, red color shows regular suffixes and bold shows prefixes for the category.

Adverbial phrase		Predicate
Noun (Point in time)	+ に　　[ni]　at	+ Verb
Noun (Point in time)	+ から　[kara]　from	+ Verb
Noun (Point in time)	+ まで　[made]　to / until	+ Verb

④ じゅぎょうは　７じに　おわります。　　[jugyoo wa shichi-ji ni owarimasu.]
The class will finish at 7 o'clock.

⑤ テストは　４じから　９じまで　です。[tesuto wa yo-ji kara ku-ji made desu.]
The test is from 4 to 9 o'clock.

⑥ ３じに　きてください。　　　　　[san-ji ni kite kudasai.]
Please come at 3 o'clock.

×⑦ ３しゅうかんに　きてください。　[san-**shuukan** ni kite kudasai.]
×Please come at 3 weeks.
(×**duration of time** + に [ni])

⑧ さんかげつ　べんきょうします。　[san-kagetsu ben'kyoo shimasu.]
I will study for 3 months.

×⑨ さんかげつに　べんきょうします。[san-**kagetsu** ni ben'kyoo shimasu]
×I will study at for 3 months.
(×**duration of time** + に [ni])

⑩ まいにち　べんきょうします。　　[mainichi ben'kyoo shimasu.]
I study everyday.

×⑪ まいにちに　べんきょうします。　[**mainichi** ni ben'kyoo shimasu.]
×I study at everyday.
(×**frequency** + に [ni])

4. Asking Time: いつ[itsu] & なんじ[nan-ji]

To ask time, we use interrogatives such as なんじ[nan-ji] and なんぷん[nan-pun], which is the combination of なん[nan] and a proper suffix (such as じ[ji] or ふん[fun]) . なん[nan] is a noun whch means 'what'. Those interrogatives are also nouns and require proper particles used together in a sentence. The interrogative いつ[itsu] (when) is also available. いつ[itsu] is an adverb by itself and does not require any suffix or particle.

⑫ なんじに　おわりますか。　　　　[nan-ji ni owarimasu ka.]
What time does it finish?
(Lit. : At what time〜?)

⑬ いつ　おわりますか。　　　　　　[itsu owarimasu ka.]
When does it finish?

×⑭ いつに　おわりますか。　　　　　[**itsu** ni owarimasu ka.]
×At when does it finish?
(×**adverb** + に[ni])

5. Demonstratives - 2

ここ[koko], そこ[soko], あそこ[asoko], and どこ[doko] are another set of こそあど [ko-so-a-do] words. They are all nouns by themselves.

こちら[kochira], そちら[sochira], あちら[achira], and どちら[dochira] are politer alternatives for them respectively. どちら[dochira] is also used for asking the name of the country, company, organisation, school which someone belongs to.

⑮ A: としょかんは どこですか。 B: そこです。
   [toshokan wa doko desu ka.   soko desu.]
   Where is the library?   It's there.

⑯ A: たなかせんせいは どちらですか。 B: あちらです。
   [Tanaka sen'see wa dochira desu ka. achira desu.]
   Where is Professor Tanaka?   She is over there.

⑰ A: だいがくは どちらですか。 B: あおぞらだいがくです。
   [daigaku wa dochira desu ka.   aozora-daigaku desu.]
   Where is your university?   It is Aozora University.

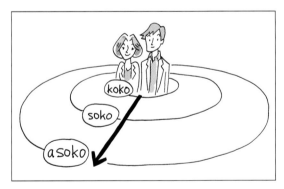

Lesson 6   Grammar Notes

《Time Expressions – 4: Calendar》

Days of the Month					
1	ついたち	[tsuitachi]	11	じゅういち　にち	[juu ichi-nichi]
2	ふつか	[futsuka]	12	じゅうに　　にち	[juu ni-nichi]
3	みっか	[mikka]	14	じゅう　よっか	[juu **yokka**]
4	**よっか**	[**yokka**]	19	じゅうく　　にち	[juu ku-nichi]
5	いつか	[itsuka]	20	**はつか**	[**hatsuka**]
6	むいか	[muika]	24	にじゅう　よっか	[nijuu **yokka**]
7	なのか	[nanoka]	26	にじゅうろくにち	[nijuu roku-nichi]
8	ようか	[yooka]	29	にじゅうく　にち	[nijuu ku-nichi]
9	ここのか	[kokonoka]	30	さんじゅう　にち	[san'juu-nichi]
10	とおか	[tooka]	?	なん　　　にち	[nan-nichi]

Days of the Week		
Sunday	にちようび	[nichi-yoobi]
Monday	げつようび	[getsu-yoobi]
Tuesday	か　ようび	[ka-yoobi]
Wednesday	すいようび	[sui-yoobi]
Thursday	もくようび	[moku-yoobi]
Friday	きんようび	[kin-yoobi]
Saturday	ど　ようび	[do-yoobi]
?	なんようび	[nan-yoobi]

Months		
January	いち　　がつ	[ichi-gatsu]
February	に　　　がつ	[ni-gatsu]
March	さん　　がつ	[san-gatsu]
April	し　　　がつ	[shi-gatsu]
May	ご　　　がつ	[go-gatsu]
June	ろく　　がつ	[roku-gatsu]
July	しち　　がつ	[shichi-gatsu]
August	はち　　がつ	[hachi-gatsu]
September	く　　　がつ	[ku-gatsu]
October	じゅう　がつ	[juu-gatsu]
November	じゅういちがつ	[juu ichi-gatsu]
December	じゅうに　がつ	[juu ni-gatsu]
?	なん　　がつ	[nan-gatsu]

— 143 —

《**Typical Japanese Sentence Structures – 3: with Various Particles**》

Topic unit	Comment unit		Predicate unit (=verb)	
	Adverbial phrase unit			
Noun + は [wa]	Noun +	Particle		
わたしは [watashi wa]	とうきょう [tookyoo] (goal / direction)	に [ni] / へ [e]	いきます [ikimasu]	。
	ちかてつ [chikatetsu] (transportation)	で [de]		
	かぞく [kazoku]	と [to]		
	ひとり [hitori]	で [de]		
	かいぎ [kaigi] (purpose)	に [ni]		
	1がつ 30にち [gatsu] [nichi] (date)	に [ni]		
	12じ [ji] (time)	に [ni]		
	10じ / ここ [ji] (time) / [koko] (place)	から [kara]		
	3じ / あそこ [ji] (time) / [asoko] (place)	まで [made]		
	コンピューター [kon'pyuutaa] (tool)	で [de]	べんきょうします [ben'kyoo shimasu]	

1. **Time Expressions - 2**

   Names of months, dates on the calendar, days of the week, and words to specify points in time (such as 'two o'clock' as studied in Lesson 5) are all nouns, which we cannot use in a sentence unless proper particles accompany them. Time expressions to show duration (such as 'two hours'), frequency (such as 'everyday') or adverbs for days (such as 'yesterday') are all adverbs by themselves that particles cannot follow as studied in Lesson 5.

   ① くがつ ついたち に おわります。
   [ku-gatsu tsuitachi ni owarimasu.]
   It finishes on September 1st.
   ② きんようび に とうきょうに いきます。
   [kin-yoobi ni tookyoo ni ikimasu.]
   I go to Tokyo on Friday.

— 144 —

× ③ まいにち に だいがくに いきます。

[**mai-nichi** ni daigaku ni ikimasu.]

× I go to the university on everyday. (×**frequency** + に [ni])

④ きのう てつやしました。

[kinoo tetsuya shimashita.]

I stayed up all night yesterday.

2. How to Make Sentences Long with Adverbs

As explained in Lesson 1, Japanese is a 'topic-comment language' and the topic unit is 'Noun＋は[wa]' which is placed at the beginning of a sentence. The shortest grammatical sentence is 'Topic (= Noun + は [wa]) + Verb'.

We can express additional information to a sentence with adverbs. Besides independent adverbs, you can make adverbial phrases by combining a noun and a particle. By adding adverbs/adverbial phrases, technically speaking, you can make infinitely long sentences. Independent adverbs and adverbial phrases are both units by themselves. The positions of those adverbs/adverbial phrases are rather free as far as you move them as units. Keep in mind that because sentences in Japanese finish with a verb, adverbs must come before the verb. Verbs always come last in the sentence, so you cannot put anything after the verb other than a question marker か [ka] or sentence ending particles such as ね [ne] and よ[yo].

⑤ わたしは (Topic) えきに くるまで きのう いきました (Predicate) 。

[watashi wa eki ni kuruma de kinoo **ikimashita**.]

I went to the station by car yesterday.

× ⑥ わたしは (Topic) 9じに えきに いきます (Predicate) まいにち 。

[watashi wa ku-ji ni eki ni **ikimasu** mainichi.]

I go to the station at 9 o'clock everyday. (×**sentence (verb)** + adverb)

— 145 —

Lesson 7 Grammar Notes

《Typical Japanese Sentence Structures – 4: with Transitive Verbs》

| Topic unit | Comment unit ||||
| | Location of action unit (=adverbial phrase) || Direct object unit || Predicate unit (=verb) |
	Noun (location)	Particle	Noun (object)	Particle	Transitive verb
わたしは [watashi wa]	レストラン [resutoran]	で [de]	ごはん [gohan]	を [o]	たべます [tabemasu] 。

1. **Transitive Sentences: Noun + を [o] + Transitive Verb**

   The particle を [o] is used to indicate the direct object of a transitive verb. In English, we indicate the direct object by where the noun is used. If we can place a noun right after a verb, the verb is a transitive verb and the noun is a direct object. In English, the word order is vital grammatical information. Therefore, if you switch subject and direct object, the sentence conveys different meaning. 'John loves Mary' and 'Mary loves John' are not the same.

   In Japanese, the direct object is indicated by the particle を [o]. 'Noun (oject) + を [o]' combination makes a direct object unit. Therefore, as long as you keep the unit, it does not matter where it is used. As for the concept of units, refer to Lesson 1. The following two sentences describe the same situation; 'I drink wine with my family'.

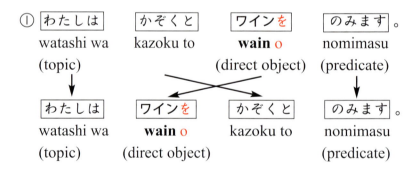

2. **Location of Action : Noun + で [de] + Action Verb**

   The particle で [de] indicates where an action took/takes/will take place. The predicate must be an action verb or a verb that describes an event.

   ② ブディさんは　うちで　ワインを　のみます。
   [Budi-san wa **uchi de** wain o nomimasu.]
   Budhi drinks wine at home.

3. **〜ませんか [〜masen ka]**

〜ませんか [〜 masen ka] is 'Negative verb form + question marker か [ka]' combination. We use it to invite someone to do something. Even though the verb is in 'negative' form, the invitation itself has a positive intention. It does not mean that the invitation itself is 'negative' (e.g. forced or unwanted).

③ A: あした　うちに　きませんか。　　[ashita uchi ni kimasen ka.]
　　　　　　　　　　　　　　　　　　　Won't you come to my place tomorrow?

　　B: いいですよ。　　　　　　　　　[ii desu yo.]
　　　　　　　　　　　　　　　　　　　Sure.

4. **〜ましょう [〜mashoo]**

〜ましょう [〜mashoo] is used to invite someone to do something together with the speaker.

You can make 〜ましょう [〜mashoo] by replacing ます [masu] in polite form of verbs with ましょう [mashoo].

We also use 〜ましょう [〜mashoo] when responding positively to an invitation or when the speaker offers to do something. The last usage will be studied later.

④ A: CDを　ききましょう。(invitation)　　[CD o kikimashoo.]
　　　　　　　　　　　　　　　　　　　　Shall we listen to a CD together?

　　B: それは　いいですね。　　　　　　[sore wa ii desu ne.]
　　　　　　　　　　　　　　　　　　　　That is good.

⑤ A: えいがを　みませんか。(invitation)　　[eega o mimasen ka.]
　　　　　　　　　　　　　　　　　　　　　Won't you watch a movie?

　　B: ええ、みましょう。(positive response)　[ee, mimashoo.]
　　　　　　　　　　　　　　　　　　　　　Sure, let's watch one.

⑥ A: カレーを　つくりましょうか。(offer)　[karee o tsukurimashoo ka.]
　　　　　　　　　　　　　　　　　　　　　Shall I make curry?

　　B: はい、ありがとうございます。　　　[hai, arigatoo gozaimasu.]
　　　　　　　　　　　　　　　　　　　　　Yes, thank you.

Lesson 8   Grammar Notes

《Typical Japanese Sentence Structures – 5: with Giving & Receiving Verbs》

Topic unit (=receiver)	Comment unit				
	Giver		Direct object		Predicate
	Noun	Particle	Noun	Particle	Verb (=to receive)
わたしは [watashi wa]	せんせい [sen'see]	に [ni]	ほん [hon]	を [o]	もらいました [moraimashita] 。

Topic unit (=giver)	Comment unit				
	Receiver		Direct object		Predicate
	Noun	Particle	Noun	Particle	Verb (=to give)
わたしは [watashi wa]	ともだち [tomodachi]	に [ni]	とけい [tokee]	を [o]	あげました [agemashita] 。

《Typical Japanese Sentence Structures – 6: with Existence Verbs》

Adverb (Location)		Subject (inanimate)		Predicate
Noun	Particle	Noun	Particle	Verb
あのビル [ano biru] そこ [soko]	に [ni]	レストラン [resutoran] コンビニ [kon'bini]	が [ga]	あります [arimasu] 。

Adverb (Location)		Subject (animate)		Predicate
Noun	Particle	Noun	Particle	Verb
だいがく [daigaku] あそこ [asoko]	に [ni]	せんせい [sen'see] いぬ [inu]	が [ga]	います [imasu] 。

《Names for Family Members》

	Yours		Someone Else's	
father	ちち	[chichi]	おとうさん	[otoo-san]
mother	はは	[haha]	おかあさん	[okaa-san]
older brother	あに	[ani]	おにいさん	[onii-san]
older sister	あね	[ane]	おねえさん	[onee-san]
younger brother	おとうと	[otooto]	おとうとさん	[otooto-san]
younger sister	いもうと	[imooto]	いもうとさん	[imooto-san]
grandfather	そふ	[sofu]	おじいさん	[ojii-san]
grandmother	そぼ	[sobo]	おばあさん	[obaa-san]
uncle	おじ	[oji]	おじさん	[oji-san]
aunt	おば	[oba]	おばさん	[oba-san]
husband	おっと / しゅじん	[otto / shujin]	ごしゅじん	[go-shujin]
wife	つま / かない	[tsuma / kanai]	おくさん	[oku-san]
children	こども	[kodomo]	おこさん	[oko-san]
son	むすこ	[musuko]	むすこさん	[musuko-san]
daughter	むすめ	[musume]	むすめさん	[musume-san]

《Demonstratives - 3》

Noun	Meaning
こんな [kon'na] + Noun 1	this kind of Noun 1
そんな [son'na] + Noun 1	that kind of Noun 1
あんな [an'na] + Noun 1	that kind of Noun 1 over there
どんな [don'na] + Noun 1	what kind of Noun 1

1. **Receiving: Noun (person)＋に[ni]＋Noun (object)＋を [o]＋もらいます [moraimasu]**
もらいます [moraimasu] indicates receiving things or information. The particle に [ni] is used to indicate from whom those things or information are received. Note that the giver cannot be the speaker. When the giver is someone superior to the receiver, いただきます [itadakimasu] is used instead of もらいます [moraimasu].

— 149 —

① ブディさんは　アンさんに　プレゼントを　もらいました。

[Budi-san wa An-san ni purezen'to o moraimashita.]

Budhi got a present from An.

×② ハインさんは　わたしに　Tシャツを　もらいました。

[Hain-san wa **watashi** ni T-shatsu o moraimashita.]

(×**speaker** + に [ni]　i.e. **speaker** ≠ giver)

③ わたしは　せんせいに　ほんを　いただきました。

[watashi wa sen'see ni hon o itadakimashita.]

I got a book from the teacher.

2. **Giving: Noun (person) + に [ni] + Noun (object) + を [o] + あげます [agemasu]**

あげます [agemasu] indicates giving things or information. The particle に[ni] is used to indicate to whom those things or information are given. Note that the receiver cannot be the speaker. When the receiver is someone superior to the giver, さしあげます [sashiagemasu] is used instead of あげます [agemasu].

④ わたしは　ともだちに　とけいを　あげました。

[watashi wa tomodachi ni tokee o agemashita.]

I gave my friend a watch.

×⑤ チンさんは　わたしに　じしょを　あげました。

[Chin-san wa **watashi** ni jisho o agemashita.]

(×**speaker** + に [ni]　i.e. **speaker** ≠ receiver)

⑥ わたしは　せんせいに　てがみを　さしあげました。

[watashi wa sen'see ni tegami o sashiagemashita.]

I gave the teacher a letter.

3. **Verbs with Implied Directions**

Some verbs show actions, which have senses of direction by nature. For example, でんわ　します[den'wa shimasu] (I make a phone call.) implies from you to someone else. てがみを　うけとります[tegami o uketorimasu] (I receive a letter.) implies from someone else to you. Even though they are not giving and receiving verbs, their actions have doers (=givers) and receivers. In sentence ⑦, the action of making a phone call is from me to the teacher. And in sentence ⑧, the action of sending an e-mail is to Budhi from An. Note that に[ni] shows both a doer (=giver) and a receiver depending on what kind of verb the sentence has.

⑦ わたしは　せんせいに　でんわを　しました。

[watashi wa **sen'see** ni den'wa o shimashita]

I made a phone call to the teacher.　　　　　　　　　I ⇒ **Teacher**

⑧ ブディさんは　アンさんに　メールを　もらいました。
　　[Budi-san wa **An-san** ni meeru o moraimashita.]
　　Budhi got e-mail from An.　　　　　　　**An** ⇒ Budhi

4. **Expressions for Existence：Noun + が [ga] + います [imasu] / あります [arimasu]**
あります [arimasu] and います [imasu] indicate the existence of a thing, person, etc. います [imasu] is used with animate subjects and あります [arimasu] is used with inanimate subjects. In order to show where something or someone is, に [ni] is used. Subject marker が [ga] used in examples ⑨ and ⑩ is introduced below.

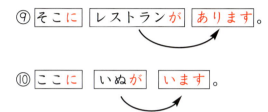

⑨ そこに　レストランが　あります。　　[soko ni resutoran ga arimasu.]
　　　　　　　　　　　　　　　　　　　　There is a restaurant there.

⑩ ここに　いぬが　います。　　　　　　[koko ni inu ga imasu.]
　　　　　　　　　　　　　　　　　　　　There is a dog here.

5. **Subject and Topic**
が [ga] is a subject marker and simply states the fact. On the other hand, は [wa] is a topic marker as we studied, and brings listeners' attention to the comment whch is following the topic. In sentence ⑪, the speaker is trying to get the listener's attention to しずおか [shizuoka] and in sentence ⑫, to ふじさん [fujisan] likewise. In short, the focus of sentence ⑪ is しずおか [shizuoka] and the one of sentence ⑫ is ふじさん [fujisan]. Therefore, sentence ⑭ is ungrammatical because the sentence has two foci (the interrogative なに [nani] and しずおか [shizuoka]). Red color in the example sentences below show foci. Interrogatives are always foci and normally a sentence has only one focus.

⑪ ふじさんは　しずおかに　あります。　[fujisan wa shizuoka ni arimasu.]
　　　　　　　　　　　　　　　　　　　　Mt. Fuji is in Shizuoka.
　　　　　　　　　　　　　　　　　　　　(Lit. As for Mt. Fuji, (it) exists in Shizuoka.)
⑫ しずおかに　ふじさんが　あります。　[shizuoka ni fujisan ga arimasu.]
　　　　　　　　　　　　　　　　　　　　Mt. Fuji is in Shizuoka.
　　　　　　　　　　　　　　　　　　　　(Lit. In Shizuoka, Mt. Fuji exists.)
⑬ ふじさんは　どこに　ありますか。　　[fujisan wa doko ni arimasu ka.]
　　　　　　　　　　　　　　　　　　　　Where is Mt. Fuji?
　　　　　　　　　　　　　　　　　　　　(Lit. As for Mt. Fuji, where does it exist?)
×⑭ なには　しずおかに　ありますか。　　[nani wa shizuoka ni arimasu ka.]
　　　　　　　　　　　×(Lit. As for what, does (it) exist in Shizuoka.)
　　　　　　　{ ×2 foci: なに [nani] and しずおか [shizuoka] ;
　　　　　　　　×Interrogative なに [nani] + **topic marker** は [**wa**]) }

6. **Nouns for Family Members**

In Japanese, it is important to distinguish between one's 'in-group' (うち [uchi]) and 'out-group' (そと [soto]). Your in-group changes depending on to whom or about whom you are talking. For example, if you are talking to your classmate about a stranger you have just met; the classmate is your in-group; the stranger is out-group. If you are talking to your mother about your classmate; however, your mother is your in-group; the classmate is out-group. This concept is so important socially in Japan where you cannot pay respect to those in your in-group. That is why we have two sets of nouns for family members as in the chart in page 149.

7. **Demonstratives - 3**

こんな [kon'na], そんな [son'na], あんな [an'na], and どんな [don'na] are another set of こそあど [ko-so-a-do] words. They are not nouns alone and must accompany a noun to make a noun phrase. Once it becomes a noun phrase, a particle can follow it. こんな [kon'na], そんな [son'na], あんな [an'na], and どんな [don'na] are used to specify types, kinds, and such of the noun they modify.

⑮ こんな　だいがくは　よくないです。　[kon'na daigaku wa yokunai desu.]
　　　　　　　　　　　　　　　　　　　　This kind of university is not good.

⑯ A：どんな　ほんを　かいましたか。　[don'na hon o kaimashita ka.]
　　　　　　　　　　　　　　　　　　　　What kind of book did you buy?

　　B：まんがを　かいました。　　　　　[manga o kaimashita.]
　　　　　　　　　　　　　　　　　　　　I bought Manga.

Study Target Index

Lesson	
Greetings	Can read his/her name, country name, and a field of study.
Greetings	Can understand and follow short and simple classroom instructions from the teacher such as "please listen""please read"if the speech is slow and clear.
Greetings	Can make basic greetings appropriate to the situation to a friend or a neighbor.
1	Can provide your own name, hometown, field of study, etc. to a person you have just met.
1	Can ask a person around you for his/her name, hometown, field of study, etc. or give such information when asked.
2	Can ask and answer to whom something belongs.
2	Can exchange phone numbers with someone.
2	Can express agreement or confirmation.
3	Can ask or answer questions about how food tastes.
3	Can make simple comments about food (e.g. 'This is good.')
3	Can ask for comments while sharing a meal with a friend.
3	Can ask if someone can eat something (e.g. 'Are you ok with…?') and answer such questions when asked.
4	Can order food or drink with simple expressions such as "this please" while pointing to a picture on a menu at a restaurant.
4	Can ask a person to do shopping for speaker or accept such request when asked.
4	Can ask a price or answer when asked.
5	Can ask the time and place of something and answer such questions when asked.
5	Can provide simple information on an item and understand such information when given.
5	Can read and understand a short, simple note written on a message board.
6	Can explain your own plan or schedule.

— 153 —

6	Can explain someone else's plan or schedule.
6	Can talk about your past experiences.
7	Can make and respond to invitations and suggestions.
7	Can discuss what to do, where to go and make arrangements to meet.
8	Can ask how people are and react.
8	Can briefly talk about your family (the number of people, member's occupations, etc.).
8	Can make comments on giving and receiving things (such as presents) and understand such comments.
8	Can greet a friend or a neighbour by mentioning the day's weather with basic expressions.

Structure Index

Lesson	
1	Particles and their Position
1	Predicate Units and their Position
1	Topic Units
1	Negative Form of です [desu]
1	Also: Noun ＋ も [mo] / Noun 1＋ も [mo] ＋ Noun 2 ＋ も [mo]
1	Questions - 1: Yes / No Question
1	Simple Answers: はい [hai] & いいえ [iie]
1	そうです [soo desu]
1	How to Connect 2 Nouns - 1
1	Saying Where You Are from
1	Concept of Units
1	Elimination of Information
2	Demonstratives - 1
2	How to Connect 2 Nouns - 2
2	Pronoun の [no] and its Elimination
2	Questions - 2 : Interrogative Questions
2	How to Tell Your Nationality
2	Sentence Ending Particles: ね [ne] ＆ よ [yo]
3	Adjectives
3	Adjectives to Modify Nouns
3	い [i] adjectives as Predicates
3	な [na] adjectives as Predicates
3	2 Kinds of です [desu]
3	Adjective Stems
3	Adjective Stem ＋ そうです [soo desu]

— 155 —

3	Adjective Stem + すぎます [sugimasu]
3	Questions - 3: Negative Questions
3	Sentence Fillers
3	Refusing with Hesitation
4	Numbers
4	Counters
4	How to Connect 2 Nouns - 3
4	Ordering Foods
5	Tense
5	Time Expressions - 1
5	Particles for Time Expressions
5	Asking Time: いつ [itsu] & なんじ [nan-ji]
5	Demonstratives - 2
6	Time Expressions - 2
6	How to Make Sentences Long with Adverbs
7	Transitive Sentences: Noun + を [o] + Transitive Verb
7	Location of Action: Noun + で [de] + Action Verb
7	〜ませんか [〜masen ka]
7	〜ましょう [〜mashoo]
8	Receiving: Noun (person) + に [ni] + Noun (object) + を [o] + もらいます [moraimasu]
8	Giving: Noun (person)＋に [ni]＋Noun (object)＋を [o] + あげます [agemasu]
8	Verbs with Implied Directions
8	Expressions for Existence: Noun + が [ga] + います [imasu] / あります [arimasu]
8	Subject and Topic
8	Nouns for Family Members
8	Demonstratives - 3

Vocabulary Index

どうし （Verbs）

Japanese	Pronunciation	English	Lesson
あいます	aimasu	to meet	8
あげます	agemasu	to give	8
あります	arimasu	(for something) to exist / there is (something) / to have (something)	8
いきます	ikimasu	to go	6
います	imasu	(for someone) to exist	8
おきます	okimasu	to wake up	5
おくります	okurimasu	to send	8
おわります	owarimasu	to finish / to end	5
かいます	kaimasu	to buy	7
かえります	kaerimasu	to return home	6
かきます	kakimasu	to write	7
かします	kashimasu	to lend	8
かります	karimasu	to borrow	8
がんばります	gan'barimasu	to hold out / to do one's best	6
ききます	kikimasu	to listen / to hear	7
きます	kimasu	to come	6
けんきゅうします	ken'kyuu shimasu	to research	6
します	shimasu	to do	7
しらべます	shirabemasu	to examine / to search / to investigate / to check out	8
じっけんします	jikken shimasu	to do an experiment	6
じゅんびします	jun'bi shimasu	to prepare	6
スピーチします	supiichi shimasu	to make a speech / give a speech	6
たべます	tabemasu	to eat	7
つくります	tsukurimasu	to make	7
てつやします	tetsuya shimasu	to stay up all night	6
でんわします	den'wa shimasu	to make a phone call	8
とります	torimasu	to take	7
ねます	nemasu	to sleep	5
のみます	nomimasu	to drink	7
はじまります	hajimarimasu	to begin / to start	5
はたらきます	hatarakimasu	to work	6
はっぴょうします	happyoo shimasu	to make a presentation	6
べんきょうします	ben'kyoo shimasu	to study	5
みます	mimasu	to watch / to see	7
メールします	meeru shimasu	to e-mail	8
もらいます	moraimasu	to receive	8
やすみます	yasumimasu	to rest	6
よみます	yomimasu	to read	7
りょこうします	ryokoo shimasu	to travel / to go on a trip	8

けいようし　(Adjectives)

Japanese	Pronunciation	English	Lesson
あたたかい	atatakai	warm	8
あたらしい	atarashii	new / fresh	4
あつい	atsui	hot	3
あまい	amai	sweet	3
いい	ii	good	3
いそがしい	isogashii	busy	3
いたい	itai	painful	8
おいしい	oishii	delicious	3
おおい	ooi	many / much	8
おおきい	ookii	big / large	3
おそい	osoi	slow / late	5
おもしろい	omoshiroi	interesting / funny	3
からい	karai	hot / spicy	3
かんたん	kan'tan	easy / simple	3
きびしい	kibishii	strict	8
きれい	kiree	beautiful / clean	8
［お］げんき	[o] gen'ki	healthy / well / peppy	8
さむい	samui	cold	8
しずか	shizuka	quiet	8
じょうず	joozu	skillful / good at (something)	8
しんせつ	shin'setsu	helpful / kind	3
すくない	sukunai	few / a little / scarce	8
すごい	sugoi	amazing / awesome	3
すずしい	suzushii	cool	8
だいじょうぶ	daijoobu	all right / fine	3
たいへん	taihen	tough (sometimes used to mean 'extremely')	3
たかい	takai	expensive	3
（せが）たかい	(se ga) takai	tall (person)	8
たのしい	tanoshii	fun / enjoyable	3
ちいさい	chiisai	small / little	3
つめたい	tsumetai	cold (to touch)	3
にぎやか	nigiyaka	bustling / busy (place) / lively / cheerful	8
ねむい	nemui	sleepy	8
はやい	hayai	fast / early	5
ひま	hima	free time	3
ふるい	furui	old	4
へた	heta	unskillful / bad at (something)	8
べんり	ben'ri	convenient	4
むずかしい	muzukashii	difficult	3
やさしい	yasashii	gentle / kind	8
やすい	yasui	cheap	3
ゆうめい	yuumee	famous	8

— 158 —

ばしょ（Places）

Japanese	Pronunciation	English	Lesson
あおぞらだいがく	aozora daigaku	Aozora University	1
あおぞらとしょかん	aozora toshokan	Aozora Library	2
あさくさ	asakusa	Asakusa	8
いざかや	izakaya	Japanese style pub	6
エスカレーター	esukareetaa	escalator	5
エレベーター	erebeetaa	elevator	5
おおさか	oosaka	Osaka	5
おおす	oosu	Osu (the name of a shopping district in downtown Nagoya)	6
おきなわ	okinawa	Okinawa	8
かいぎしつ	kaigi-shitsu	conference room / meeting room	5
かいだん	kaidan	staircase	5
カフェ	kafe	café	5
～かん	～kan	～building (counter for large buildings)	6
かんこうち	kan'koochi	tourist spot	8
かんこく	kan'koku	South Korea	1
きょうしつ	kyooshitsu	classroom	5
きょうと	kyooto	Kyoto	6
ぎんこう	gin'koo	bank	5
くやくしょ	ku-yakusho	ward office	7
コンビニ	kon'bini	convenience store	4
さかえ	sakae	Sakae (the name of shopping district in downtown Nagoya)	6
じっけんしつ	jikken-shitsu	laboratory	5
じむしつ	jimu-shitsu	office	5
しやくしょ	shi-yakusho	city hall	7
しょくどう	shokudoo	dining hall / cafeteria / canteen	5
スーパー	suupaa	supermarket	6
せいきょう	seekyoo	Co-op store	4
タイ	tai	Thailand	1
だいがく	daigaku	university	1
ちか	chika	basement	5
ちゅうがっこう	chuugakkoo	Junior high school	6
ちゅうごく	chuugoku	China	1
トイレ(おてあらい)	toire (o-tearai)	toilet / rest room	5
とうきょう	tookyoo	Tokyo	6
としょかん	toshokan	library	5
なごや	nagoya	Nagoya	8
２ごうかん	ni-gookan	building 2	6
にっしんだい	nissin dai	Nisshin Uni	1
にっしんだいがく	nisshin daigaku	Nisshin University	1
にほん	nihon	Japan	1

Index　ごいインデックス Vocabulary Index

Japanese	Pronunciation	English	Lesson
にゅうかん	nyuukan	immigration	7
ばいてん	baiten	stand / campus store	4
パンや	pan-ya	bakery	5
びょういん	byooin	hospital	7
ビル（たてもの）	biru (tatemono)	building	5
ふじさん	fuji-san	Mt. Fuji	6
ふじやまえき	fujiyama eki	Fujiyama Station	2
ふるさと	furusato	hometown	8
ベトナム	betonamu	Vietnam	1
へや	heya	room	5
ほっかいどう	hokkaidoo	Hokkaido	5
ほんや	hon-ya	book store	5
マレーシア	mareeshia	Malaysia	1
ゆうびんきょく	yuubin'kyoku	post office	5
レストラン	resutoran	restaurant	6
ロビー	robii	lobby	5

たべもの・のみもの　（Foods & Drinks）

Japanese	Pronunciation	English	Lesson
あさごはん	asa-gohan	breakfast	7
アイスコーヒー	aisu koohii	iced coffee	4
アイスティー	aisu tii	iced tea	4
おかし	o-kashi	sweets	5
おちゃ	o-cha	tea	4
おにぎり	onigiri	rice ball	3
カップラーメン	kappu raamen	cup noodles	4
カフェラテ	kafe rate	cafe latte	4
からあげ	kara'age	deep fried chicken	3
キャンディー	kyan'dii	candy	5
ぎゅうどん	gyuudon	beef bowl	3
クッキー	kukkii	cookie	5
ケーキ	keeki	cake	3
コーヒー	koohii	coffee	4
コーラ	koora	cola	4
ごはん	gohan	meal	7
［お］さけ	[o] sake	alcohol	7
サンドイッチ	san'doicchi	sandwich	4
ジュース	juusu	juice	4
［お］すし	[o] sushi	sushi	3
たべもの	tabemono	food	3
チーズバーガー	chiizu baagaa	cheese burger	4
チョコレート	chokoreeto	chocolate	5
テリヤキバーガー	teriyaki baagaa	teriyaki burger	4
にくまん	nikuman	steamed bun with pork filling	3
ハンバーガー	han'baagaa	hamburger	4
ビール	biiru	beer	7
ピザ	piza	pizza	7
ばんごはん	ban-gohan	dinner	7
ひるごはん	hiru-gohan	lunch	7
フライドチキン	furaido chikin	fried chicken	3
ホットチキン	hotto chikin	spicy chicken	3
マンゴー	man'goo	mango	7
みそしる	miso shiru	miso soup	3
ワイン	wain	wine	7
わがし	wagashi	Japanese sweets	3
わさび	wasabi	wasabi	3

さくいん
Index by Hiragana sounds

hiragana	pronunciation	Lesson	hiragana	pronunciation	Lesson
1 じ	ichi-ji	5	あのひと（あのかた）	ano hito (ano kata)	1
2 じ	ni-ji	5	あまい	amai	3
3 じ	san-ji	5	あまり	amari	3
4 じ	yo-ji	5	あめ	ame	8
5 じ	go-ji	5	ありがとうございます	arigatoo gozaimasu	Gre.
6 じ	roku-ji	5	あります	arimasu	8
7 じ	shichi-ji	5	あるいて	aruite	6
8 じ	hachi-ji	5	あれ	are	2
9 じ	ku-ji	5			
10 じ	juu-ji	5	**＜い＞**		
11 じ	juuichi-ji	5	いい	ii	3
12 じ	juuni-ji	5	いいえ	iie	1
5 ふん	go-fun	5	いいです	ii desu	Gre.
10 ぷん	jip-pun / jup-pun	5	いいですか	ii desu ka	4
2 ごうかん	ni-gookan	6	いきます	ikimasu	6
			いくつ	ikutsu	4
＜あ＞			いくら	ikura	4
あ	a	1	いざかや	izakaya	6
ああ	aa	2	いしゃ	isha	8
アイスコーヒー	aisu koohii	4	いす	isu	2
アイスティー	aisu tii	4	いそがしい	isogashii	3
あいます	aimasu	8	いたい	itai	8
あおぞらだいがく	aozora daigaku	1	いただきます	itadakimasu	3
あおぞらとしょかん	aozora toshokan		いただきます	itadakimasu	5
あげます	agemasu	8	いち	ichi	2
あさ	asa	6	いつ	itsu	6
あさくさ	asakusa	8	いつか	itsuka	6
あさごはん	asa-gohan	7	いっしょに	issho ni	4
あさって	asatte	5	いっしょにどうですか	issho ni doo desu ka	6
あした	ashita	5	いつつ	itsutsu	4
あそこ	asoko	5	いってきます	ittekimasu	4
あたたかい	atatakai	8	いってください	itte kudasai	Gre.
あたらしい	atarashii	4	いつも	itsumo	7
あちら	achira	5	いぬ	inu	8
あつい	atsui	3	いま	ima	5
あに	ani	8	います	imasu	8
あね	ane	8	いもうと	imooto	8
あの	ano	1	いらっしゃいませ	irasshaimase	4
あの〜	ano〜	2	いんせい	in'see	1

— 162 —

hiragana	pronunciation	Lesson
＜う＞		
うーん	uun	3
うち	uchi	5
うちあわせ	uchiawase	5
うみ	umi	8
＜え＞		
ATM	eetiiemu	5
えいが	eega	7
えいご	ee-go	2
ええ	ee	4
えーっと	eetto	4
エスカレーター	esukareetaa	5
えっ!?	e!?	4
エレベーター	erebeetaa	5
～えん	～en	4
えんぴつ	en'pitsu	2
＜お＞		
おいしい	oishii	3
おおい	ooi	8
おおきい	ookii	3
おおさか	oosaka	5
おおす	oosu	6
おかし	o-kashi	5
おきなわ	okinawa	8
おきます	okimasu	5
おきゃくさま	o-kyaku-sama	4
［お］くに	[o] kuni	5
おくります	okurimasu	8
［お］げんき	[o] gen'ki	8
［お］さけ	[o] sake	7
［お］すし	[o] sushi	3
おそい	osoi	5
おちゃ	o-cha	4
おつかれさまでした	otsukaresama deshita	5
おとうと	otooto	8
おととい	ototoi	5
おなまえは？	o-namae wa?	5
おにぎり	onigiri	3
おねがいします	onegaishimasu	Gre.
おねがいできますか	onegai dekimasu ka	4
おはようございます	ohayoo gozaimasu	Gre.
おみせのひと	o-mise no hito	4

hiragana	pronunciation	Lesson
おみやげ	o-miyage	5
おもしろい	omoshiroi	3
おわりましょう	owarimashoo	Gre.
おわります	owarimasu	5
おんがく	on'gaku	7
＜か＞		
カード	kaado	8
～かい（がい）	～kai (gai)	5
かいぎ	kaigi	5
かいぎしつ	kaigi-shitsu	5
かいしゃいん	kaishain	8
かいだん	kaidan	5
かいてください	kaite kudasai	Gre.
かいます	kaimasu	7
かえります	kaerimasu	6
かがく	kagaku	1
かぎ	kagi	2
かきます	kakimasu	7
がくせい	gakusee	1
かさ	kasa	2
かします	kashimasu	8
かしこまりました	kashikomarimashita	4
カタカナ	katakana	3
がっかい	gakkai	6
カップラーメン	kappu raamen	4
かばん	kaban	2
カフェ	kafe	5
カフェラテ	kafe rate	4
かようび	ka-yoobi	5
～から	～kara	6
～から　きました	～kara kimashita	1
からあげ	kara'age	3
からい	karai	3
カラオケ	karaoke	6
かります	karimasu	8
～かん	～kan	6
かんげいパーティ	kan'gee paatii	3
かんこうち	kan'koochi	8
かんこく	kan'koku	1
かんたん	kan'tan	3
がんばってください	gan'batte kudasai	5
がんばります	gan'barimasu	6

— 163 —

hiragana	pronunciation	Lesson	hiragana	pronunciation	Lesson
＜き＞			**＜こ＞**		
きいてください	kiite kudasai	Gre.	～ご	～go	2
ききます	kikimasu	7	ご	go	2
きてください	kite kudasai	Gre.	こいびと	koibito	8
きのう	kinoo	5	こうかんりゅうがくせい	kookan ryuugakusee	1
きびしい	kibishii	8	こうぎ	koogi	5
きます	kimasu	6	こうこうせい	kookoosee	8
キャンディー	kyan'dii	5	コーヒー	koohii	4
きゅう／く	kyuu / ku	2	コーラ	koora	4
ぎゅうどん	gyuudon	3	[ご] かぞく	[go] kazoku	7
きょう	kyoo	5	こくさいかんけい	kokusai kan'kee	1
きょういく	kyooiku	1	ここ	koko	5
きょうかしょ	kyookasho	2	ごご	gogo	5
きょうし	kyooshi	8	ここのか	kokonoka	6
きょうしつ	kyooshitsu	5	ここの　がくせい	koko no gakusee	1
きょうと	kyooto	6	ここのつ	kokonotsu	4
きょねん	kyo-nen	6	ごぜん	gozen	5
きれい	kiree	8	こたえ	kotae	Gre.
ぎんこう	gin'koo	5	ごちゅうもんは？	go-chuumon wa?	4
きんようび	kin-yoobi	5	こちら	kochira	5
			こちらは～さんです	kochira wa～san desu	1
＜く＞			ことし	kotoshi	6
～ください	～kudasai	4	この～	kono～	2
クッキー	kukkii	5	ごはん	gohan	7
くやくしょ	ku-yakusho	7	コピー	kopii	2
くらい（ぐらい）	kurai [gurai]	4	これ	kore	2
クラス	kurasu	5	これから　いっしょに	korekara issho ni	
クリスマス	kurisumasu	8	けんきゅう　します	ken'kyuu shimasu	1
くるま	kuruma	6	こんげつ	kon-getsu	6
			こんしゅう	kon-shuu	6
＜け＞			こんど	kon'do	7
けいざい	keezai	1	こんにちは	kon'nichiwa	Gre.
ケーキ	keeki	3	こんばん	kon-ban	6
ケータイ	keetai	2	こんばんは	kon'banwa	Gre.
ゲーム	geemu	7	コンビニ	kon'bini	4
けさ	kesa	6	コンピューター	kon'pyuutaa	1
げつようび	getsu-yoobi	5			
けんきゅう	ken'kyuu	2	**＜さ＞**		
けんきゅういん	ken'kyuuin	1	さあ	saa	3
けんきゅうかい	ken'kyuu-kai	6	さかえ	sakae	6
けんきゅうしつ	ken'kyuushitsu	6	さしあげます	sashiagemasu	5
けんきゅうします	ken'kyuu shimasu	6	ざっし	zasshi	2
けんきゅうせい	ken'kyuusee	1	さむい	samui	8
けんしゅうりょこう	ken'shuu ryokoo	6	さようなら	sayoonara	Gre.

— 164 —

hiragana	pronunciation	Lesson	hiragana	pronunciation	Lesson
〜さん	〜san	1	**＜す＞**		
さん	san	2	すいようび	sui-yoobi	5
サンドイッチ	san'doicchi	4	すうがく	suugaku	2
			スーパー	suupaa	6
＜し＞			すくない	sukunai	8
CD	shiidii	2	スケジュール	sukejuuru	3
じこしょうかい	jiko shookai	1	すごい	sugoi	3
じしょ	jisho	2	すずしい	suzushii	8
しずか	shizuka	8	スター・ウォーズ	sutaa uoozu	7
じっけん	jikken	5	スピーチします	supiichi shimasu	6
じっけんしつ	jikkenshitsu	5	スマホ	sumaho	2
じっけんします	jikken shimasu	6	すみません	sumimasen	Gre.
じっしゅう	jisshuu	5			
しつもん	shitsumon	Gre.	**＜せ＞**		
しつれいします	shitsuree shimasu	Gre.	せ	se	8
しつれいですが…	shitsuree desu ga...	1	せいかつ	seekatsu	3
〜してください	〜shite kudasai	Gre	せいきょう	seekyoo	4
じてんしゃ	jiten'sha	6	(せが) たかい	(se ga) takai	8
じどうはんばいき	jidoo han'baiki	5	ぜひ	zehi.	7
します	shimasu	7	ゼミ	zemi	2
じむしつ	jimushitsu	5	せん	sen	4
じむのひと	jimu no hito	1	せんげつ	sen-getsu	6
じゃ	ja	4	せんしゅう	sen-shuu	6
じゃ、また	ja, mata	Gre.	せんせい	sen'sei	1
シャープペンシル	shaapu pen'shiru	2	せんぱい	sen'pai	1
しやくしょ	shi-yakusho	7	ぜんぶで	zen'bu de	4
しゃしん	shashin	7	せんもん	sen'mon	1
じゅう	juu	2			
ジュース	juusu	4	**＜そ＞**		
じゅうよっか	juuyokka	6	そう	soo	1
じゅぎょう	jugyoo	5	そうですか	soo desu ka	1
しゅくだい	shukudai	Gre.	そうですね	soo desu ne	7
じゅんびします	jun'bi shimasu	6	そこ	soko	5
じょうず	joozu	8	そして	soshite	5
しょくどう	shokudoo	5	そちら	sochira	5
じょしゅ	joshu	1	その〜	sono〜	2
しらべます	shirabemasu	8	それ	sore	2
しりょう	shiryoo	2	それから	sorekara	7
〜じん	〜jin	1	それは いいですね	sore wa ii desu ne	7
しんかんせん	shin'kan'sen	6			
しんせつ	shin'setsu	3	**＜た＞**		
しんぶん	shin'bun	2	タイ	tai	1
			だいがく	daigaku	1
			だいがくいんせい	daigakuin'see	1

— 165 —

hiragana	pronunciation	Lesson	hiragana	pronunciation	Lesson
だいがくせい	daigakusee	8	てんきよほう	ten'ki yohoo	8
だいじょうぶ	daijoobu	3	でんしじしょ	den'shi jisho	2
たいへん	taihen	3	でんしゃ	den'sha	6
たかい	takai	3	でんわ	den'wa	2
タクシー	takushii	6	でんわします	den'wa shimasu	8
たこやき	takoyaki	8	でんわばんごう	den'wa ban'goo	2
ただいま	tadaima	4			
たのしい	tanoshii	3	<と>		
たべます	tabemasu	7	～と	～to	7
たべもの	tabemono	3	トイレ（おてあらい）	toire (o-tearai)	5
だれ（どなた）	dare (donata)	1	どう	doo	3
たんじょうび	tan'joobi	8	とうきょう	tookyoo	7
			どうぞ	doozo	3
<ち>			[どうぞ] よろしく	[doozo] yoroshiku	
ちいさい	chiisai	3	[おねがいします]	[onegaishimasu]	1
チーズバーガー	chiizu baagaa	4	どうも　ありがとう	doomo arigatoo	2
ちか	chika	5	どうも	doomo	5
ちがいます	chigaimasu	Gre.	とお	too	4
ちかてつ	chikatetsu	6	とおか	tooka	6
チケット	chiketto	3	ドクター	dokutaa	1
ちち	chichi	8	とけい	tokee	2
ちゅうがっこう	chuugakkoo	6	どこ	doko	5
ちゅうごく	chuugoku	1	ところ	tokoro	8
チョコレート	chokoreeto	5	としょかん	toshokan	5
ちょっと	chotto	3	どちら	dochira	5
ちょっと…	chotto…	3	とても	totemo	3
			ともだち	tomodachi	2
<つ>			どようび	do-yoobi	5
ついたち	tsuitachi	6	とります	torimasu	7
つかれました	tsukaremashita	5	どんな	don'na	8
つくえ	tsukue	2			
つくります	tsukurimasu	7	<な>		
つめたい	tsumetai	3	なごや	nagoya	8
			なつやすみ	natsu-yasumi	8
<て>			なな／しち	nana / shichi	2
Tシャツ	T-shatsu	5	ななつ	nanatsu	4
DVD	diibuidii	7	なに	nani	8
てがみ	tegami	7	なのか	nanoka	6
てつやします	tetsuya shimasu	6	なまえ	namae	Gre.
デパート	depaato	5	なん	nan	2
でも	demo	8	なんがい	nan-gai	5
テリヤキバーガー	teriyaki baagaa	4	なんがつ	nan-gatsu	6
テレビ	terebi	7	なんじ	nan-ji	5
てんき	ten'ki	8	なんじに	nan-ji ni	6

hiragana	pronunciation	Lesson	hiragana	pronunciation	Lesson
なんで	nan de	6	はち	hachi	2
なんて　かいて	nan'te kaite		はつか	hatsuka	6
ありますか	arimasu ka	5	はっぴょう	happyoo	2
なんにち	nan-nichi	6	はっぴょうします	happyoo shimasu	6
なんにん	nan-nin	8	はな	hana	8
なんばん	nan-ban	2	はは	haha	8
なんぷん	nan-pun	5	はやい	hayai	5
なんようび	nan-yoobi	5	はれ	hare	8
			はん	han	5
<に>			ばん	ban	6
に	ni	2	ばんごはん	ban-gohan	7
にぎやか	nigiyaka	8	ハンバーガー	han'baagaa	4
にくまん	nikuman	3	パンや	pan-ya	5
にじゅうよっか	nijuuyokka	6			
にちようび	nichi-yoobi	5	<ひ>		
にっしんだい	nisshin dai	1	ビール	biiru	7
にっしんだいがく	nisshin daigaku	1	ひこうき	hikooki	6
にほん	nihon	1	ピザ	piza	7
にほんご	nihon-go	2	ひさしぶりですね	hisashiburi desu ne	8
にゅうかん	nyuukan	7	ひと	hito	8
〜にん	〜nin	8	ひとつ	hitotsu	4
にんぎょう	nin'gyoo	5	ひとり	hitori	7
			ひとり	hitori	8
<ね>			ひま	hima	3
ねこ	neko	8	ひゃく	hyaku	4
ねます	nemasu	5	びょういん	byooin	7
ねむい	nemui	8	ひらがな	hiragana	3
〜ねん	〜nen	6	ひる	hiru	6
			ビル（たてもの）	biru (tatemono)	5
<の>			ひるごはん	hiru-gohan	7
ノート	nooto	2	ひるやすみ	hiru-yasumi	6
のみます	nomimasu	7			
			<ふ>		
<は>			ふじさん	fujisan	6
パーティー	paatii	3	ふじやまえき	fujiyama eki	2
はい	hai	1	ふたつ	futatsu	4
ばいてん	baiten	4	ふたり	futari	8
はじまります	hajimarimasu	5	ふつか	futsuka	6
はじめまして	hajimemashite	1	ぶっか	bukka	8
はじめましょう	hajimemashoo	Gre.	ぶつり	butsuri	1
ばしょ	basho	5	ふゆやすみ	fuyu-yasumi	8
バス	basu	6	フライドチキン	furaido chikin	3
パソコン	pasokon	2	ふるい	furui	4
はたらきます	hatarakimasu	6	ふるさと	furusato	8

— 167 —

hiragana	pronunciation	Lesson	hiragana	pronunciation	Lesson
プレゼント	purezen'to	8	**＜む＞**		
			むいか	muika	6
＜へ＞			むずかしい	muzukashii	3
へえ	hee	2	むっつ	muttsu	4
へた	heta	8			
ベトナム	betonamu	1	**＜め＞**		
へや	heya	5	めいてつ	meetetsu	6
べんきょう	ben'kyoo	3	メール	meeru	8
べんきょうします	ben'kyoo shimasu	6	メールします	meeru shimasu	8
べんり	ben'ri	4	メモ	memo	5
＜ほ＞			**＜も＞**		
ほうがく	hoogaku	1	もう	moo	5
ぼうし	booshi	8	もういちど	moo ichido	Gre.
ぼく	boku	1	もうすぐ	moosugu	8
ボールペン	boorupen	2	もくようび	moku-yoobi	5
ほっかいどう	hokkaidoo	5	もらいます	moraimasu	8
ホットチキン	hotto chikin	3			
ほん	hon	2	**＜や＞**		
ほんや	hon-ya	5	やさしい	yasashii	8
			やすい	yasui	3
＜ま＞			やすみ	yasumi	5
まいあさ	mai-asa	6	やすみましょう	yasumimashoo	Gre.
まいにち	mainichi	3	やすみます	yasumimasu	6
まいばん	mai-ban	6	やっつ	yattsu	4
マスター	masutaa	1			
まだ	mada	5	**＜ゆ＞**		
まつり	matsuri	7	ゆうびんきょく	yuubin'kyoku	5
～まで	～made	6	ゆうめい	yuumee	8
マナカ	manaka	2	ゆき	yuki	8
マレーシア	mareeshia	1			
まん	man	4	**＜よ＞**		
マンゴー	man'goo	7	ようか	yooka	6
			よっか	yokka	6
＜み＞			よっつ	yottsu	4
みそしる	miso shiru	3	よみます	yomimasu	7
みっか	mikka	6	よん / し	yon / shi	2
みっつ	mittsu	4	よんでください	yon'de kudasai	Gre.
みてください	mite kudasai	Gre.			
みなさん	mina-san	3	**＜ら＞**		
みます	mimasu	7	らいげつ	rai-getsu	6
みんな	min'na	6	らいしゅう	rai-shuu	6
			らいねん	rai-nen	6

hiragana	pronunciation	Lesson	hiragana	pronunciation	Lesson
＜り＞			**＜ろ＞**		
りゅうがくせい	ryuugakusee	1	ろく	roku	2
りょう	ryoo	2	ロビー	robii	5
りょうしん	ryooshin	8			
りょうり	ryoori	8	**＜わ＞**		
りょこうします	ryokoo shimasu	8	わあ！	waa!	3
			ワイン	wain	7
＜れ＞			わがし	wagashi	3
れい	ree	Gre.	わかりました	wakarimashita	Gre.
レジュメ	rejume	2	わかりますか	wakarimasu ka	Gre.
レストラン	resutoran	6	わかりません	wakarimasen	Gre.
レポート	repooto	2	わさび	wasabi	3
			わたし	watashi	1

さくいん

Index by Hiragana sounds

Structual Exercises : writing

こたえ

Lesson 1

1.

1) アンさんも　いんせいですか。

2) ハインさんは　にほんじん じゃ ありません。

3) わたしは　マレーシアから　きました。

4) ジョンさんは　にっしんだいがくの　だいがく
 いんせい です。

2.

1) あんどうさん、あんどうさん、いんせい、じょしゅ

2) ミンさん、タイ、ミンさん、ベトナム

3) そう、コンピューター、ぶつり

4) たかはし、だいがくいんせい、コンピューター

5) ハイン、ベトナム、ほうがく

Lesson 2

1.

1) あれは　ぶつりの　ざっし　です。

2) それは　なん　ですか。

3) それは　タンさんの　じしょ です。

4) アンさんの　でんわばんごうは　なんばんです
 か。

2.

1) わたし、だれ、もりさん

2) なん、せんもん、だれ

3.

1) せんもん、ハインさん

2) はっぴょう、しりょう、いいえ、ブディさん

3) たかはしさん、　レポート

4.

1) だれの

2) なんの

3) なんばん

5.

1)　よ　　2) ね　　3)　か

Lesson 3

1.

1) この　からあげは　おいしいです。

2) あの　かばんは　おおきいです。

3) その　ほんは　どうですか。

4) タンさんは　とても　しんせつです。

5) あの　とけいは　たかそうです。

Answers

Lesson 1

1.

1) An-san mo in'see desu ka.

2) Hain-san wa Nihon-jin ja'arimasen.

3) Watashi wa Mareeshia kara kimashita.

4) Jon-san wa Nisshin Daigaku no daigakuin'see desu.

2.

1) Andoo-san, Andoo-san, insee, joshu

2) Min-san, Tai, Min-san, Betonamu

3) Soo, kon'pyuutaa, butsuri,

4) Takahashi, daigakuinsee, kon'pyuutaa

5) Hain, Betonamu, hoogaku

Lesson 2

1.

1) Are wa butsuri no zasshi desu.

2) Sore wa nan desu ka.

3) Sore wa Tan-san no jisho desu.

4) An-san no den'waban'goo wa nan'ban desu ka.

2.

1) watashi, Dare, Mori-san

2) nan, Sen'mon, Dare

3.

1) sen'mon, Hain-san

2) Happyoo, shiryoo, Iie, Budi-san

3) Takahashi-san, repooto

4.

1) dare no

2) nan' no

3) nan'ban

5.

1) yo 2) ne 3) ka

Lesson 3

1.

1) Kono kara'age wa oishii desu.

2) Ano kaban' wa ookii desu.

3) Sono hon wa doo desuka.

4) Tan-san wa totemo shin'setsu desu.

5) Ano tokee wa takasoo desu.

2.

1) どう、むずかしい

2) いそがしい、 たいへん

3) おいしそう、おいしい

4) どうぞ、どう

3.

1) はい、おもしろいです。

2) いいえ、からくないです。

3) はい、だいじょうぶです。

4.

1) どう　2) どう　3) なん、どう

Lesson 4

1.

2	ふたつ	3	みっつ	4	よっつ
5	いつつ	6	むっつ	7	ななつ
8	やっつ	9	ここのつ	10	とお

2.

100	ひゃく	200	にひゃく
300	さんびゃく	600	ろっぴゃく
800	はっぴゃく	1,000	せん
3,000	さんぜん	8,000	はっせん
10,000	いちまん		
6,400	ろくせん　よんひゃく		
89,700	はちまん　きゅうせん　ななひゃく		

3.

1) チーズバーガー、みっつ　おねがいします。

2) コーヒーと　サンドイッチ、おねがいします。
　　（サンドイッチと　コーヒー、おねがいします。）

3) ぜんぶで　いくら　ですか。

4.

1) ばいてん、ふたつ、いくら、ぜんぶ、400えん

2) あの、えっ、Ｃさん、ありがとう

Lesson 5

1.

1) ぎんこうは　ごぜん　8じから　です。

2) 1じはんに　きて　ください。

3) ばいてんの　やすみは　にちようび　です。

4) これは　マレーシアの　おみやげ　です。

5) くじから　じゅういちじ　まで　べんきょうし
　　ます。

2.

1) doo, muzukashii

2) isogashii, taihen

3) oishisoo, oishii

4) doozo, Doo

3.

1) Hai, omoshiroi desu.

2) Iie, karakunai desu.

3) Hai, daijoobu desu.

4.

1) doo　2) doo　3) nan, doo

Lesson 4

1.

2	futatsu	3	mittsu	4	yottsu
5	itsutsu	6	muttsu	7	nanatsu
8	yattsu	9	kokonotsu	10	too

2.

100	hyaku	200	ni hyaku
300	san byaku	600	rop pyaku
800	hap pyaku	1,000	sen
3,000	san zen	8,000	has sen
10,000	ichi man		
6,400	roku sen yon hyaku		
89,700	hachi man' kyuu sen nana hyaku		

3.

1) Chiizu-baagaa, mittsu onegaishimasu.

2) Koohii to san'doicchi, onegaishimasu.
　（San'doicchi to koohii, onegaishimasu.）

3) Zen'bu de ikura desu ka.

4.

1) Baiten, futatsu, Ikura, Zenbu, 400-en

2) Ano, E, C-san, Arigatoo

Lesson 5

1.

1) Gin'koo wa gozen 8-ji kara desu.

2) 1-ji han ni kite kudasai.

3) Baiten no yasumi wa nichi-yoobi desu.

4) Kore wa Mareeshia no omiyage desu.

5) 9-ji kara 11-ji made ben'kyoo shimasu.

— 171 —

2.

1) はじまります、おわります

2) ごぜん、ごご、から、まで

3.

1) なんじ　　　2) なんじ

3) なんようび　4) どこ

4.

1) じむしつ、はちじはん、ごご　ごじ、
　　どようび、にちようび

2) どこ

5.

1) おかし、きょうと

2) れい）タイ　おみやげ

Lesson 6

1.

1) まいにち　くじに　だいがくに　いきます。

2) バスで　ゆうびんきょくに　いきます。

2.

1) バス　けんしゅうりょこう

2) でんしゃ　だいがく

3) しんかんせん　ふじさん

4) ひこうき　ほっかいどう

3.

1) なんで　2) なんで　3) いつ

4.

1) クラス、にほんご、じゅうじ

2) けんきゅうかい、くるま、いっしょ

5.

1) にがつに　はっぴょうしました

2) さんがつに　かえります

3) じゅうにがつ　はつか、いちがつ　むいか

6. れい）

1) 10じに　ねました。

2) 7じに　おきました。

3) ちかてつで　きました。

4) ともだちの　うちに　いきます。

5) らいねんの　3がつに　かえります。

6) 10がつ　15にちです。

Lesson 7

1.

1) こんど　コンサートに　いきませんか。

2) いっしょに　しゃしんを　とりましょう。

3) うちで　ピザを　たべました。

4) チンさんと　がっかいに　いきました。

2.

1) hajimarimasu, owarimasu

2) gozen, gogo, kara, made

3.

1) nan-ji　　　2) nan-ji

3) nan-yoobi　　4) doko

4.

1) jimushitsu, Hachi-ji han, Gogo go-ji,
　　Doyoobi, nichi-yoobi

2) doko

5.

1) O-kashi, Kyooto

2) e.g.) Tai, o-miyage

Lesson 6

1.

1) Mainichi ku-ji ni daigaku ni ikimasu.

2) Basu de yuubin'kyoku ni ikimasu.

2.

1) basu kenshuu ryokoo

2) den'sha, daigaku

3) shin'kan'sen Fuji-san

4) hikooki Hokkaidoo

3.

1) Nan de 2) Nan de 3) Itsu

4.

1) kurasu, Nihon-go, 10-ji

2) ken'kyuu-kai, kuruma, issho

5.

1) ni-gatsu ni happyoo shimashita

2) san-gatsu ni kaerimasu

3) Juuni-gatsu hatsuka, ichi-gatsu muika

6. e.g.)

1) 10-ji ni nemashita.

2) 7-ji ni okimashita.

3) Chikatetsu de kimashita.

4) Tomodachi no uchi ni ikimasu.

5) Rainen no 3-gatsu ni kaerimasu.

6) 10-gatsu 15-nichi desu.

Lesson 7

1.

1) Kon'do konsaato ni ikimasen ka.

2) Issho ni shashin o torimashoo.

3) Uchi de piza o tabemashita.

4) Chin-san to gakkai ni ikimashita.

2.

1) いきます、なんで、じてんしゃ
2) ともだち、うち、えいが、ビール
3) たべませんか、たべますか、いきませんか、 いきましょう
4) やすみます、いきます、わかりました

3.

1) を　2) で、を　3) で、に　4) に

4. れい)

1) ラーメンを　たべました。
2) サッカーを　します。
3) せんせいに　あいました。
4) としょかんで　します。

Lesson 8

1.

1) とうきょうは　にぎやかな　ところです
2) わたしの　かぞくは　4にん　です
3) ははは　ほっかいどうに　います
4) あには　やさしいひと　です
5) このかばんは　ともだちに　もらいました

2.

1) あります　　　　　　2) います
3) あります　　　　　　4) います、います
5) に、を　　　　　　　6) で、を
7) に、を

3.

1) いそがしい　　　　　2) さむい
3) ゆうめいな　　　　　4) たかい
5) げんきな

4.

1) なんにん、りょうしん、とうきょう、がくせい
2) ふたり、つま、かいしゃいん
3) あたたかい、てんき、ゆき、さむい
4) やすみ、でんわ、わかりました

5.

1) ともだちに　おくります。
2) こいびとに　もらいました。
3) せんぱいに　かります。

6. れい)

1) うみが　きれいな　ところです。
2) ふじさんが　ゆうめいです。
3) はい、おいしいです。すしが　おいしいです。
4) くだものが　たかいです。パンが　やすいです。
5) ともだちに　メールします。
6) ははに　あげます。
7) ①とけいを　もらいました。
　　②ちちに　もらいました。

2.

1) ikimasu, Nan de, Jiten'sha
2) tomodachi, uchi, eega, biiru
3) tabemasenka, tabemasu ka, ikimasen ka, ikimashoo
4) yasumimasu, ikimasu, Wakarimashita.

3.

1) o　2) de, o　3) de, ni　4) ni

4.

1) Raamen o tabemashita.
2) Sakkaa o shimasu.
3) Sen'see ni aimashita.
4) Toshokan de shimasu.

Lesson 8

1.

1) Tokyoo wa nigiyakana tokoro desu
2) Watashi no kazoku wa 4-nin desu
3) Haha wa Hokkaidoo ni imasu
4) Ani wa yasashii hito desu
5) Kono kaban wa tomodachi ni moraimashita

2.

1) arimasu　　　　　　2) imasu
3) arimasu　　　　　　4) imasu, imasu
5) ni, o　　　　　　　6) de, o
7) ni, o

3.

1) isogashii　　　　　2) samui
3) yuumeena　　　　4) takai
5) gen'kina

4.

1) nan-nin, ryooshin, Tookyoo, gakusee
2) futari, Tsuma, kaishain
3) atatakai, ten'ki, Yuki, samui
4) yasumi, den'wa, Wakarimashita

5.

1) Tomodachi ni okurimasu.
2) Koibito ni moraimashita.
3) Senpai ni karimasu.

6. e.g.)

1) Umi ga kireina tokoro desu.
2) Fuji-san ga yuumee desu.
3) Hai, oishiidesu. Susiga oishii desu.
4) Kudamono ga takai desu. Pan ga yasui desu.
5) Tomodachi ni meeru shimasu.
6) Haha ni agemasu.
7) ①Tokee o moraimashita.
　　②Chichi ni moraimashita.

かいとう　Answers (Structual Exercises : writing)

留学生の　サバイバル日本語 1
SURVIVAL JAPANESE FOR UNIVERSITY STUDENTS 1

著　者 ©

徳 本　浩 子
名古屋外国語大学　国際日本語教育インスティテュート准教授

山 本　裕 子
愛知淑徳大学　交流文化学部教授

鈴 木 かおり
名古屋外国語大学　国際日本語教育インスティテュート非常勤講師
小牧市国際交流協会　日本語教室・プレスクール主任講師

録音協力
森　幸長
名古屋学芸大学　メディア造形学部映像メディア学科講師

イラスト
アンドウカヲリ

著者承認検印廃止

2017年 4月10日　初版発行

定価本体　2,600 円 (税別)

発行者　山　崎　雅　昭
印刷所　音 羽 印 刷 株 式 会 社
製本所　有限会社 壺屋製本所

発行所 早 美 出 版 社
東京都新宿区早稲田町80番地
郵便番号162-0042
TEL. 03(3203) 7251　FAX. 03(3203)7417
振替　東京 00160-3-100140

ISBN978-4-86042-086-4 C3081 ¥2600E
http://www.sobi-shuppansha.com

こっき [kokki] Flags

 にほん[nihon] Japan
 ちゅうごく[chuugoku] China
 かんこく[kan'koku] Korea

 フィリピン[firipin] Phillippines
 ベトナム[betonamu] Vietnam
 タイ[nihon] Thai

 マレーシア[mareeshia] Malaysia
 インドネシア[in'doneshia] Indonesia
 トルコ[toruko] Turkey

 オーストラリア[oosutoraria] Australia
 ニュージーランド[nyuujiiran'do] New Zealand

 イギリス[igirisu] England
 フランス[furan'su] France
 ドイツ[doitsu] Germany

 イタリア[itaria] Italy
 スペイン[supein] Spain
 オランダ[oran'da] The Netherlands

 ベルギー[berugii] Belgium
 ロシア[roshia] Russia

 エジプト[ejiputo] Egypt

 アメリカ[amerika] U.S.A.
 カナダ[kanada] Canada
 メキシコ[mekishiko] Mexico

 ブラジル[burajiru] Brazil
 ペルー[peruu] Peru
 アルゼンチン[aruzen'chin] Argentina

いろ [iro] Colours

 あか[aka]
 あお[ao]
 くろ[kuro]
 しろ[shiro]

 きいろ[kiiro]
 ちゃいろ[chairo]
 みどり[midori]
 ピンク[pin'ku]

 みずいろ[mizuiro]
 グレー[guree]